Silence, Nc

CW01466177

By

April Humphreys

Table of Contents

ACKNOWLEDGMENTS

I would like to say a huge thank you to Claire, my editor, for helping shape the words that tell my story. When your life reads like mine, it's very hard to trust and believe in anyone, but it has to be said that Claire has proved to have the biggest heart and the sweetest soul, restoring my faith in human nature. She has been passionate, totally committed to her work, and stands by her beliefs with a genuine fierceness to be admired. She has stepped into my mind in the most incredible way, making this an extremely surreal experience, one that will tie us together forever going forward.

Thank you to my cousins Hannah, Teddy, and Jerry, who never judged me and believed me without question. Thank you to Jerry for 'keeping me on your radar.'

Thank you to my girls for the unwavering support they have shown me throughout their entire lives, now joined by their husbands. Thank you for providing me with four amazing grandchildren whose lives I am blessed to be a part of and who have shown me what true love is.

And most of all, I would like to thank my husband, Jim. Without him, I would not be here to write this story. There are no words to express just how much I truly love him and appreciate him being my 'rock.' If there is a 'God,' he for sure sent Jim my way. So, I thank God, too.

I thank ALL of you for making my life worth living.

PROLOGUE

Prologue: The Letters

It's late 2023. The house is quiet, the kind of quiet that happens when everyone is away, and there's nothing but the hum of the fridge and the soft ticking of the clock. I sit at the dining room table, a cup of tea with just a dash of milk cooling beside me, fingers resting on the iPad. I've been here for over an hour now, staring at the screen, thinking about the words I'm about to write.

The letters.

My gaze drifts to the window, where the November sky is a dull grey, typical for this time of year. It's strange how the weight of the past can hang in the air like that, heavy, thick, and invisible. No one else can see it, but it's there, pressing down on me as I try to find a way to explain years of absence. Years of silence.

A small sneeze and then a nudge at my leg. Toffee, my 14-year-old Pug/King Charles Cross, looks up at me with wide, hopeful eyes, her tail wagging softly against the floor. She wants attention, of course. If the phrase 'look at me!' were embodied in a dog, it would be Toffee. She *demands* attention, whether it's through excited yips, insistent nudges, or just staring at you with those big, pleading brown eyes until you acknowledge her contenting presence. I smile down at her, my hand twitching to reach out and pet her, but I know better. If I give in to Toffee, even for a second, I'll lose focus.

"Later, Toffee," I murmur, my voice soft. She lets out a small huff, plopping down at my feet in exaggerated defeat.

I can feel the warmth of her leaning against my leg, her presence a comfort, even though I know I must stay in the moment.

I take a slow breath, trying to calm the nerves fluttering in my stomach. It's not the writing that's hard. I've written letters hundreds of times before. But these letters are different. These are the ones that will crack open everything I've been holding back for so long.

It's funny, I think, how the decision to write these letters seemed clear. But now, sitting here, I feel that familiar tug of doubt. Maybe it would be easier to leave it all unsaid. To continue as I have for years: distant, polite, absent from family gatherings, but safe. Safe in my silence.

But that's the problem. The silence has never felt safe. It's been like being a chained animal in a cage, never experiencing true freedom. Now those chains are about to be unlocked and the cage door opened, and I'd be dealing with a completely different world.

I push my fingers against the keys, tapping out a sentence, then deleting it. Then trying again. How do you begin a conversation that will change everything? How do you tell people who have known you your whole life that they don't really know you at all? I think about my relatives, Hannah, Faith, others who've probably wondered why I'm never around anymore. They probably think I'm a cold person and that I simply don't care.

I reach for my tea and take a sip. Cold. I sit the cup back down, staring at the blinking cursor.

It's not that I don't care. It's that I care too much.

The truth about why I've stayed away, why I've been quiet, is messy and dark. And it's tied to a past I've tried to forget, my father, the house, the things that happened that no one ever talked about. For years, I convinced myself that it was easier to keep quiet, to let the distance grow between me and the rest of the family. It was simpler that way. But now, sitting here, fingers resting on the iPad, I know the silence has been anything but simple.

I start typing, not overthinking the words this time.

When I finish, I only re-read it a couple of times – unusual for me. I can agonise over the right words to say to the postman! *I'm doing this for me*, I remind myself. I'm ready to break the silence. Ready to explain why I've been absent, why I couldn't be part of the family in the way it may have been expected. I end the letter with 'you can email me at april********@gmail.com.'

I send the letter to Jim, who prints off some copies, and I put them into envelopes ready to post.

It's done.

I lean back in my chair, my hands dropping into my lap. Toffee, ever attuned to my moods, nudges my leg gently, her warm eyes searching mine. This time, I reach down and run my fingers through her soft fur, grateful for her steady presence over the past 14 years. She's been my quiet anchor, loving, loyal, and always there when the weight of the past felt unbearable. I think of Rascal, my other little dog, a Shih Tzu-Lhasa mix, whose absence still makes me sad in quiet moments like this. They've both been there for me in ways words can't capture. But this, this moment, is a journey of the heart, one only I can take.

I posted the letters, and I waited.

For days, I checked my email, trying not to feel that familiar pang of anxiety each time there was nothing new. And then, one afternoon, a notification pops up on my phone. An email from Hannah and Teddy!

I open it, my breath catching slightly.

Hi April, It was such a shock to receive your letter and we can't imagine what it must have been like for you over all these years. We would like to meet with you when you are ready. Either you can come here or we can come to you, or if you prefer, as you are close to the nature reserve, we could meet there, weather permitting, please just let us know. Hope to hear from you soon, Hannah & Teddy xxxxx

I stare at the words, my chest tight, but not in the way I'm used to. It's not fear or dread this time. It's something softer. A kind of relief. Hannah doesn't sound like she thinks I'm making it up or that I'm overreacting.

Another email comes in, this time from Faith.

Dear April, I want you to know I read your letter in shock several times with tears running down my face. I want you to know that there is absolutely no judgement. I am horrified and absolutely furious with what you have suffered. I've read it to Richard, who obviously is in shock. I also want you to know there is no question at all that we believe you...

The rest of the email blurs as I blink back tears. I hadn't expected this. I hadn't expected to be believed. After so many years of holding everything inside, of feeling like no one would understand, here were two people, two people who *mattered*, telling me they believed me.

For the first time in a long time, I realised the silence didn't have to define me anymore. The letters and the responses I received were my validation after so many years of feeling unheard. And then I thought, if writing those letters could bring me such a sense of freedom, what could writing a book do? How might sharing my story help others who have been through the same?

That question stayed with me. And this book is my answer.

PART ONE

CHAPTER ONE

An Unwanted Arrival

December, 1962

I don't know much about the house where I was born. All I know is that my parents started off in a tiny bedsit, and when the landlady found out my mother was expecting my brother – their first child – the landlady threw them out. How they managed to get the house I was born in, I do not know. All I know is that it was rented.

It was December of 1962, and Britain was swallowed up by the coldest winter in two hundred years. Snowdrifts outside our door rose as high as my mother's waist, she would say, and each gust rattled the old windowpanes like icy hands trying to claw their way in. Mum would also tell me countless times that I was an accident, as casually as if she were reminding me to wear a hat in the cold. The words were always the same; only her tone varied, a careless shrug whenever someone asked about me. I was born in that winter, pulled into the world in Westfield Road, Hornsey, London. I was told that it was a big house, but I cannot imagine it was a home with many comforts, with no crib waiting, no blankets. They hadn't expected me, so my cradle became a drawer yanked from an old chest, padded with sweaters that likely still smelled of mothballs.

1

Uncle Bill came over the morning after I was born, his big boots crunching across the icy path. Uncle Bill was nothing short of lovable and funny. He never married or had children of his own, but by the time I came along, he'd already welcomed a niece and a few nephews.

Apparently, he leaned down, his face close to mine, his voice raspy. "Looks like a screwed-up prune, doesn't she?" I imagine the scratchy laughter that followed, and the way his words hung in the air, joking. It was just an observation, a wrinkled prune.

In our family, words were often weapons as much as tools. Even kindness was delivered with a sting, a subtle insult disguised as a compliment. And so, from my very first hours, I was exposed to a quiet indifference. This was now home.

*****

February, 1990

Twenty-eight years later, I found myself walking home after an evening at a neighbour's house. The night air was cold and crisp, with the stillness of winter, a silence that felt almost sacred. But that quiet didn't last. A howling, a guttural sound that cut through the silence, stopped me in my tracks. My next-door neighbour stood in his front garden, his face twisted with something I couldn't pinpoint; something primal and terrifying. I felt my stomach drop. He screamed, and begged me to go inside with him, to see something he couldn't face alone. But I wasn't able to do it. I didn't know why then, but something deep inside told me not to go. I had learned to trust my instincts after years of constantly living on the edge of fear.

2

Another neighbour, braver or more oblivious, answered the call. I watched from the safety of my own doorstep as the police tape went up, cordoning off the house where four children had once lived, laughed, and played. Now, it was a crime scene, and the police were asking to use our phone because they couldn't touch anything inside.

"Forensics," they said.

It was then that I overheard a police officer on the phone, her voice clinical, almost detached, as she relayed the horror that had unfolded next door. "The four children have been garrotted," she said. I didn't know the word at the time, but its weight was unmistakable. I felt sick.

That night, as the police led the mother away in handcuffs, she kept repeating, "I told the doctor what I was going to do! I told him. I told him what I was going to do!"

Her voice was chillingly calm, as though discussing something as mundane as a shopping list. A few days later, the news broke that the doctor had been struck off. But it didn't matter. Nothing mattered, not the press that swarmed our doorstep the following day, not the sympathetic whispers from neighbours who didn't know what to say. All I could think about were those four little bodies lying cold and still in their beds just a few feet away from where I slept.

The next day, I called my mother, seeking some semblance of comfort or understanding. But when I told her what had happened, her response was just as cold as ever.

"Things happen much closer to home than that," she said, as though dismissing the tragedy next door as a mere inconvenience. I felt something inside me break all over again. How could she make light of something so horrific?

3

What hope did I have that she'd ever understand me, my pain, the reality of my childhood?

I took a breath, steadied myself and said, "Things have happened closer to home, Mum."

But as always, her non-response swallowed my words whole.

****

I'm at the bottom of a deep, cold, dark hole. The air feels thick, and the shadows close in, smothering every flicker of light. I shout for help, but all I hear is the echo of my own voice bouncing off the walls, growing louder and louder, tormenting me. The sound is relentless, and it's all I can hear. It's maddening, pushing me to the brink, where I just want to scream, desperate to find some way to shut it all off.

Why am I the only one who hears these cries? Why doesn't anyone else? I'm just a child, lost in this bewildering, bleak world, with nowhere to turn and no one to help me understand.

These nightmares still haunt me.

But now, it's time to climb out of that cold, dark hole. Time to rise into the light, into the warmth of a sunny day, and stand mountain tall, where everyone can see me. I am no longer invisible, small, or defenceless. I hold a loudspeaker in my hand, and I *will* be heard, whether they like it or not. I am standing up to my abusers, and I refuse to be silenced again. It is the present day; I am 61 years old, and for the first time, I am *truly* free. I am finally the person I was always meant to be: *heard and counted.*

But before I can truly let go of these nightmares that I have endured for almost six decades, I must tell my story. I will not be silenced.

My silence is NOT for sale.

*****

As a very young child, I knew no different. When I was told to "touch this, kiss this, put this in your mouth", I did as I was told. The thing was *hideous*; it smelt like fish, and it tasted even worse, like wee, if I had to imagine what wee tasted like! The first time it happened, I had no idea what would happen next. He made me hold the thing in my mouth, and then he pulled and pushed my head, back and forth, back and forth, to show me what he wanted me to do. It felt like it would never end. I had a ragdoll at the time, and I likened the flimsiness of the ragdoll's movement to mine as he pushed and pulled at me. I didn't understand why this was happening; *all I knew was that I hated it.* Just when I thought it couldn't get any worse, I was told to "pick up speed", and as I did, that thing would go so far into my tiny mouth that it hit the back of my throat, making me gag.

And then, to my ultimate horror, he released something foul into my mouth. I thought he had weed – I didn't understand ejaculation at that age. He then said, "If you swallow it, I'll give you extra pennies for sweets." I was so relieved just to have that thing out of my mouth, if only for a little while. But that relief was always short-lived.

My childhood was spent in a state of dread, knowing that it would happen again and again. I often felt numb, struggling to find any enthusiasm or purpose in life, because I knew that sooner or later, I'd be back in that horrible place, enduring it all over again.

I didn't even know knocking on a door before entering was a thing. I would lie in bed, staring at that bedroom door, dreading the moment it might open. As I watched it, I realised that the way it was designed to offer a small sense of privacy was a built-in warning. Whoever entered had to walk around the door before they could even see into the room.

Why, then, did I always feel the need to hide just behind it, desperate for a sliver of my own privacy? Most of the time, I'd retreat to the bathroom, where the small lock offered a brief sense of security. It didn't matter whether I was getting dressed or undressed; I was always positioned right behind that door, bracing myself, hoping that the element of surprise might make him hesitate long enough to walk away.

This "father", *my* father, was not a dad; he was a monster that lurked around every corner and could be felt in the darkest of nights. To the outside world, he was a hard-working pillar of the community. He had "living a double life" down to an art.

He, along with my mother, was successful in silencing me for many years. Unfortunately, for my abusers, those days are over. I will not be silenced any longer.

This is my story.

CHAPTER TWO

The Bait

My first ever childhood memory. The garage door groaned open, casting long shadows. The air hung heavy with the smell of motor oil. I was just a child, my hand dwarfed in my father's grip. He led me to the back corner, a single bare lightbulb casting a low glow.

He crouched down, his face uncomfortably close.

A bar of Caramac, its shiny gold wrapper glinting in the dim light, appeared as if by magic.

Mum always used to joke that I didn't eat a thing for the first three days of my life, but I never stopped eating after that! Chocolate, the sweet nectar of the gods, sat proudly at the top of my favourite food pyramid.

There, in the garage, my father opened his trousers and presented me with his penis. I didn't know that word at the time. I perhaps knew it as "a willy" at best.

"Touch this for me, and you can have this bar of Caramac," he said.

I don't remember what went through my mind at that time; after all, I was so small, and this was a completely novel request.

I did as he said. I must have blocked some of this "first experience", as my memory stops there.

What I can remember, however, is the sweet, milky richness of the chocolate immediately after.

It sends shivers down my spine to imagine someone exposing themselves to me now – the horror! But back then, the lines between right and wrong were smudged like a toddler's finger painting. Innocence and ignorance were my armour. Hindsight is a funny thing, isn't it? Because now, it's painfully obvious.

I took the bait.

The next memory is a stark contrast. Bright sunlight streaming through the kitchen window, the smell of toast. My mother's hands, gentle but firm, pulling long white socks up my chubby legs. I was obviously too young to do it myself. I must have understood in some primal way that what my father had done was somehow wrong, because I clearly remember trying to tell Mum about the incident. As I began to explain what had happened in the garage with my father, her face hardened, and the realisation of the horrifying truth hit the expression on her face. I thought she would go on to offer words of comfort, but then came the words that would dictate how I operated in the world from that point forward.

"Don't you EVER speak of that again!" she said, looking me deep in the eyes.

She hurried me along; my maternal grandparents were about to arrive soon. It's obvious to me now that such subjects brought shame and disgrace to people's door, but of course I didn't understand her dismissal at the time. What I had said was not the sort of thing Mum wanted broadcasted to others or, especially, to hear for herself.

It was Mum's words in that moment that normalised the secrecy of the abuse for me. From there on in, I understood that the abuse was to be endured and never spoken of. None of the other children at school mentioned such happenings. In my young mind, I thought it was obvious that all children lived a replica life to me and that every child was given the same rules to follow. After all, kids did what they were told in those days!

Well, I did, anyway.

Shame smothered the words in my throat. It became our secret, my father's and mine. I grew up believing that this was just how things were. That fathers did these things, and mothers pretended not to know. That children kept secrets, even from themselves.

After the garage incident, my father became a regular, unwelcome visitor to me. Things escalated very quickly, and before I knew it, my father's willy being shoved down my tiny throat became an every-other-day occurrence, in the shadows, where nobody could help me.

He often told me that if I was to swallow, I would get extra pennies to buy sweets. When I was five years old in the 1960s, 10 pennies got you a great deal of sweets!

My love for my mother was fierce, even when she was sharp and distant. I believed she was trapped, afraid to leave, as scared as I was. I feel sorry for the little girl who thought she had allies in this scary situation. Looking back, I see the flaws in my logic, the warped loyalty that kept me silent. But in those days, it was all I knew.

One of the hardest things I faced was my mum's absolute lack of sensitivity towards the subject. It was as if she had this knack for stepping on my emotions without worrying about the damage she was causing. I became an expert at biting my tongue, forcing myself to stay quiet just to avoid yet another confrontation. Time and time again, I'd stand there, suppressing the urge to defend myself, wishing I had the courage to say the words that always seemed stuck. After every hurtful conversation, I'd replay it in my mind, imagining all the things I should have said, thinking, "Why didn't I speak up?" or "I should have set her straight." That regret gnawed away at me; each missed opportunity was a reminder of how trapped I felt.

As the years went by, Mum, who should have known better, had an uncanny way of constantly offending me. What stung the most was how easily she could sweep everything under the rug, especially when it came to Father and the terrible things he was doing. She buried it so deep, it was as if it wasn't happening or hadn't ever happened.

She could even make flippant remarks about abuse, utterly detached from the reality of our home. Once, after watching something on TV, she turned to me and said, "*It's disgusting, isn't it? What some people do to their own families!*"

The sheer hypocrisy of it left me overwhelmed and speechless.

If she had just switched the channel over, it would have been less offensive. The way she did it, you couldn't blame me for thinking that she was actually trying to rub my nose in it. In reality, she didn't care enough to think that deeply about it, and it just became another offhand remark.

In fact, life with my mother felt like one long, offhand remark! I was like the runt of the litter, treated as such. She never noticed me clinging to her, never stopped to ask why

I didn't want to be left alone with my father or why I dreaded car journeys with him alone. She seemed perfectly content to insist I be there or go, no matter the circumstances. To me, every action she took and every word she said twisted the knife a little deeper, and over the years, it just got worse and worse.

In later years, I remember she once told me a joke about two dogs and actually used the word "incest" in the punchline. Needless to say, I didn't find her joke funny.

Playing "happy families" was more than just a game; it was *survival*. God forbid that I could ever show, inside or outside the home, the effects the sexual abuse was having on me. The rules of their game were simple but relentless: say and do exactly what Mother and Father wanted. Be the version of yourself that fit *their* expectations, or you'd find yourself cast out from the family, isolated. It felt like walking on eggshells every single day. One wrong word, one wrong action, and I'd be on the outside, cut off from the very people I was bending over backwards to please. The suffocation of it wrapped around me, squeezing the life out of all my thoughts, my emotions, and my *real* self.

The effort it took to maintain the façade drained every last bit of strength I had. It wasn't just about biting my tongue in the heat of the moment; it was about reprogramming my entire way of being. Every instinct that screamed for me to stand up against the abuse, every truth I wanted to speak, had to be silenced, buried beneath layers of compliance. I was constantly turning my thoughts inside out, pretending to be someone else, just to survive the day.

Given that I knew no different, I truly believed that the terrifying things going on in my home were simply normal and that all children were going through similar things in *their* homes. It was exhausting, mentally, emotionally, and physically, because despite my beliefs, it wasn't something, as a child, my young mind could process or make sense of. Feeling terrified might seem normal when it's all you've ever known, but that familiarity does nothing to lessen how utterly, unbelievably harrowing it is every single time. I just had to go along with whatever was presenting itself, which in my case was my father's fucking penis!

Year after year, as I grew from a five-year-old in that garage, I fought this internal battle, all to protect the person I loved most – Mum.

I convinced myself that if I just did everything Mother wanted — one day she would recognise the sacrifices I made. I carried that hope like a shield, yearning for the day she'd see me. *Truly* see me, and finally thank me for protecting her, for doing what I thought was best. I didn't know how long I might have to wait, but still I held on to the hope, clutching it with both hands, even as it slipped further and further from my grasp. Even as the weight of it became unbearable, I couldn't let go of the fact that one day, all the pain and suffering would mean something to her. That one day, she'd see what it had cost me to play their game so well.

CHAPTER THREE

The Sanctuary Next Door and a Guardian With Fur

On birthdays, Mum had this little ritual, one that felt like magic. She'd sneak into our room in the middle of the night, leaving presents at the foot of our bed. The idea was that we'd wake in the morning, and it was as if the presents had simply appeared while we slept. I remember waking up in the middle of the night on my fifth birthday, my heart skipping with excitement when I spotted the gift – a Tiny Tears doll – sitting there in the moonlight. She was perfect, dressed in the loveliest clothes, all thanks to our next-door neighbour, Mrs Flemming. The doll even came with her own little carrycot and bedding.

Mrs Flemming, with her gentle hands and kind eyes, had sewn a tiny blue coat for my new baby doll. It had pearl buttons, a delicate lace collar, and beneath it, the doll wore a lace nightie, every stitch placed with care. I adored that Tiny Tears; it could drink imaginary milk, suck on a dummy, and even wet itself. I treated it like my own little baby, so maternal already, even at such a young age.

Mrs Flemming was more than a neighbour to me. In my childish imagination, I believed she had special powers, that one day she'd see through the walls and find out what was happening behind closed doors. It was a comforting fantasy, one that helped me feel less alone. She was my safety net, even if it was only in my mind.

13

Mum loved Mrs Flemming too, but for different reasons. Gardening was their shared passion. It became Mum's escape from the house, from us, and from the responsibilities she never seemed to want. She would spend hours out there, tending to her plants, lost in the world she and Mrs Flemming had created. Our gardens were linked by a little wooden gate, and I loved wandering through it, feeling like I was stepping into another world.

Mrs Flemming's garden was smaller than ours, but it felt so much bigger, so much richer. It was alive with colour and smells, especially the sweet peas. Every year, they climbed up her greenhouse, and I can still see her now, snipping them for a vase inside, their scent lingering in the air like summer itself. The greenhouse was on the left side of the garden, and a winding path curved around it, leading to a magnificent cherry tree. That tree was the heart of the garden, its branches heavy with fruit, enough for everyone to share. It stood like a silent witness to all the life that happened beneath it.

The path continued past a pond, but not just any pond; it was huge, or at least it felt that way to me. Its knee-high wall was the perfect spot to perch and watch the koi fish swim in lazy circles. To my young eyes, they were enormous, almost otherworldly. Mrs Flemming would often fret about the herons that tried to steal them, but the pond remained unfazed, like everything else in her garden.

Inside her house, I would sit for what seemed like hours watching the fish in their tank in the armchair that sat beside it. Such a contrast in size to those outside in the pond. Their soft movements were soothing, almost hypnotic.

Inside her house, however, Mr Flemming, her husband, was the opposite of soothing. He was a man of few words, most of them grumbled under his breath. Maybe because it was *his* chair I was sitting in. It was a comfy chair, I had to admit, the kind that seemed to beckon you to sink in and never leave. I could see why he was so attached to it.

I was never at their house to visit him though. It was always Mrs Flemming I sought out for her warmth and kindness. At Christmas, we'd go next door, almost before breakfast, for a sherry, a tradition Mum insisted on. I remember one year, Mrs Flemming gave me a tiny china angel. I took it as a sign, convincing myself that it meant help was coming. But tiny china angels, as it turns out, can't see through walls, and neither could Mrs Flemming.

Reality always had a way of creeping back in. I learned early on that I couldn't rely on anyone to save me. Even with all the imagination in the world, there were some things that remained too dark to change.

Religion wasn't a part of our home, as Mum and Father didn't have time for it. They even used to condemn Father's favourite sister Rose for being so obsessed with God, but somehow, I ended up attending Sunday school. That's probably where I got my own small Bible. I remember writing in it, promising to keep it with me always, to take it with me when I died. Looking back, it feels like the desperate act of a child searching for hope, for something to hold on to when everything else felt drained and empty.

Mum used to say that Father was more sociable than she was, and maybe that was true in some ways. But that didn't stop them both from having a full social life, leaving me to find comfort wherever I could, whether in Mrs Flemming's garden, beside the pond, or simply in the world I built inside my own head.

Loneliness settled into the cracks of my life and in the shadows of our home. Only my father and I knew the full truth of what was really happening. Mother had decided to completely ignore it.

But one day, a small reprieve came. My mother, who had always been fond of animals, took me along on one of her Avon rounds, where she would sell makeup and perfumes door to door. There was a surprise waiting for me that day. One of her customers was rehoming a dog, and Mum had said "yes" to taking her - just like that! That's how Cindy came into our lives.

My first memory of Cindy is as clear as day. We were driving home in Mum's little Mini, the car my father had surprised her with at Christmas. That car was her pride and joy. Father couldn't fit the real car under the Christmas tree, so he wrapped up a tiny matchbox version of a Mini instead. I remember the excitement when she unwrapped it and the disbelief when she realised what that little toy car meant.

In the back of that Mini, my eyes met Cindy's for the first time. She was staring at me with this big, ugly Boxer face, tongue lolling out, panting as if she'd run a marathon. If you've ever seen a Boxer pant, you'll know it's not exactly love at first sight! But there was something about her that drew me in. She was awkward, rough around the edges, and yet somehow perfect. I didn't know it then, but I was going to love that dog more than I ever thought possible.

Cindy's early days with us weren't smooth sailing. One day, I came home from school to find Mum frantically stitching up our leather sofa. Cindy had taken her boredom out on the cushions, shredding it like prey. Whether it was the scent of the leather or just mischief, she'd done a proper number on it. Mum was desperate to patch things up before Father came home, knowing full well that he would go mad if he saw the destruction. It was only the beginning of Cindy's escapades.

Mum had this old-fashioned gold-coloured tea trolley, which was probably very trendy at the time, that she wheeled out when we had guests over – usually Aunt Flo and Uncle Ernie. I vividly remember the night humans first landed on the moon, July 20, 1969, and the excitement buzzing in the room. But my focus wasn't on the TV; it was on Mum's trolley. She'd load it up with a pot of tea, cups, saucers, teaspoons, and, on the lower shelf, treats like cheese and onion pastries and perfectly sliced Victoria sponge cake.

That evening, before the trolley even made it into the living room, a slice of cake mysteriously vanished. We were baffled until we turned around and saw Cindy, her face smeared with cream, the missing slice still hanging from her mouth. She'd helped herself without anyone noticing. She pulled the same trick at Christmas with a Yule log. It didn't help that all the food was conveniently at her eye level.

Father's pride and joy was his immaculate lawn. He tended to it as if it were a living, breathing entity, each blade of grass carefully nurtured, watered, and trimmed with obsessive precision. He would tell Mother that the lawn 'was the largest plant in the garden'. That lawn was his, and nothing was allowed to disrupt it. Cindy, naturally, was forbidden from stepping a paw onto his sacred green. She

17

seemed to understand the invisible line that separated the patio from his precious turf, and with a single stern word from him, she'd freeze in her tracks, instinctively knowing better than to push her luck.

I used to dress Cindy up in all sorts of ridiculous outfits: bikinis, Mum's old tights stretched over her head like a burglar mask. Once, I even spoon-fed her porridge while she lay back, looking as if she belonged on a throne.

But what I *truly* loved was when she'd set upon Father.

Cindy had this habit of cornering him in his chair, barking and growling wildly as though she were confronting him with all the things no one else could see. Watching him panic, shouting for Mum, "Get a newspaper, Jo!" as he tried to swat Cindy away with a rolled-up paper, was the most joy I ever felt in that house. I believe Cindy saw him for what he *truly* was, even when nobody else could.

Animals, as I've learnt over the years, have a way of sensing things we often try to bury. They pick up on the unspoken tensions, the things unsaid. And when you've lived through the kind of trauma I have, you begin to feel like a trapped, helpless creature in your own home. That's how I felt: like a defenceless animal, constantly on edge, bracing for the next time Father would shove his penis into my little mouth or his hands down my knickers.

Cindy wasn't allowed on the beds, but my brother often let her sneak onto his when no one was looking, even taking photos of her lounging where she wasn't supposed to be. Those photos always landed him in trouble, but I think the rebellion was worth it.

I don't remember Cindy falling ill, not in any obvious way. But one day, I came home, and she was gone. Just like that. My parents told me she'd been "diagnosed with throat cancer" and had to be put to sleep. No warning, no chance to say goodbye. I was heartbroken, devastated that the only soul in that house who had ever truly understood me was gone without a word.

Cindy was more than a dog; she was a quiet protector in a world that often felt hostile. I didn't get to say "thank you" or "I love you" to her for the last time, and maybe that's the way life works, taking things from you without warning, just as it does with people who should have protected you but didn't. But Cindy left me with something far more valuable than memories: she showed me what loyalty, instinct, and unspoken love look like. In a house that I found to be scary, Cindy was a light, and even after she was gone, her presence stayed with me, reminding me of a truth I was only just beginning to understand myself. That there are bad people in the world, there are good people, and there are those in the middle. But both dogs and frightened little girls can sense the bad people a mile off.

CHAPTER FOUR

Mum and the Garden

The first thing I remember about my mother is the way she smoked. Before even getting out of bed in the morning, my father would bring her a cup of tea, a chocolate biscuit, and her first cigarette of the day. She wouldn't even sit up, just reach over to the side table, lighting it with the same practiced ease as breathing. She never smoked a whole cigarette in one go. Instead, she would take a few drags, then carefully pinch the end and rest it on the edge of the ashtray, only to relight it later. Over and over, all day long. More than anything, I remember the ritual of it, watching her endlessly lighting up half-smoked "dog ends", the faint curl of smoke always in the air.

She had smoked since she was twelve, and I had never known her without the scent of tobacco clinging to her clothes. But the smell of stale smoke clinging to her clothes and breath never stopped me from wanting to be close to her. I would inch closer, despite the stale scent of smoke, drawn by her presence, desperate for any scrap of affection she might unknowingly offer. Funnily enough, Mum never wore deodorant, but I can't recall her ever smelling bad; maybe it was just part of her that I accepted without question. I would often find her at the bathroom sink, stripped down to her "cross-your-heart" bra and those infamous Bridget Jones knickers, washing under her arms with a flannel, always with coal tar soap. Mum was particular about her privacy when dressing, but oddly enough, she never seemed to mind me being around when she washed or when she was sat on the toilet. I realise now just how much I shadowed her, always within arm's reach, as if proximity to her could somehow keep me safe.

It wasn't unusual to find her perched on the toilet, arms resting on her knees, cigarette in hand, puffing away like it was the most normal thing in the world. She sat in her armchair the same way, arms resting on her knees, cigarette smouldering, watching war films on the telly after cooking the Sunday roast. After selfishly serving herself the crispiest roast potatoes, she'd send us kids off across the road for sweets and settle into her comfy chair, eyes glued to the screen. She loved anything with a bit of violence, Romans battling, soldiers at war; if it involved fighting, Mum was all in.

Mum devoured war films, fascinated by battles and suffering in faraway places. When it was Auschwitz, she'd shake her head and mutter, *"Those heinous crimes should never be forgotten."* Yet somehow, she had no trouble forgetting the one that was happening in her own home.

How could she say that when she was so willing to forget the evil crime being forced upon *me*?

Each time those words left her lips, *"Those heinous crimes should never be forgotten,"* they carried the same sharp sting.

How could she feel such outrage about atrocities that happened so far away, so long ago, yet remain indifferent to the prison and torture house my own father had built right within our home?

It baffled me. It outraged me.

When Mum needed to escape the world, she'd disappear into the garden, not because it was beautiful or particularly inviting, but because it was *hers*. Mrs Fleming's garden was lovely, a place that felt alive, but ours was different. I was only six weeks old when we moved into that house, so I have no memory of what the garden looked like back then. There's an old photo, though, a snapshot of tangled shrubs and bushes that were meant to stay, to give us secret places to play and hide. But that's not how it turned out.

Instead, the garden became something else: less of a playground, more of a blank canvas. A small pond, a patio added here and there, but it felt unfinished, like it was waiting for something. And really, that garden wasn't for kids. It was for *her*. Mum's flowerbeds ran the length of the garden, carefully maintained, stretching out as far as her mind needed to wander. It felt less like a place of joy for us and more like her private retreat from everything else. The garden wasn't for us; it was the only place where she was truly alone, where no one could demand anything of her. It was hers and hers alone. A place where she could retreat and control, a quiet corner of the world that was all hers, and she could find peace.

While she was still alive, Cindy, our dog, was always stationed on the patio, held there by nothing more than Father's stern command to not touch his lawn. She never needed a lead; his voice was enough. Cindy's reward for her loyalty was often a pig's trotter, one of those cheap staples that filled our kitchen cupboards. Mum had a knack for making everything stretch, buying whole animals, like half a lamb or a whole pig, to keep us fed; it was when chest freezers had just been introduced. Mother was privileged enough to have an upright one. Aunt Bet, Mum's sister, even made brawn from the pig's head, though that was one line Mum wouldn't cross.

If Mum was in the greenhouse, you'd usually find me right there beside her, probably making mudpies while she tended to her plants. I was like a puppy, never far from her heels. Back then, tortoises seemed to be *everywhere*, and somehow, we ended up with seven. Some were found, others given. The smallest one I named Tarzan. Father had made a small, fenced area down the side of her greenhouse, just a foot wide, and that became their first home. Eventually, he built them little houses under one of the apple trees in the garden. I remember those houses, with their arched doorways, carefully crafted by him. He even drilled tiny holes in the tortoises' shells, tying string to them so they wouldn't wander off. When winter came, they were packed up in straw, tucked into a cardboard box, and shelved in my father's shed. Every spring, we'd peer into the box, holding our breath, hoping maggots hadn't got to them.

My father's shed was a marvel of its own. Stone-clad, with a smaller covered area attached, where he stored long pieces of wood from various jobs. In front, there was a stack of rabbit hutches, layered high like a little tower. It was common for the rabbits to have babies, and we'd peek into the corners of the cages, looking for tiny new arrivals. But we had to be careful; if the mother sensed we'd been near, she'd kill her own babies. That idea horrified me. I remember naming them all: Bubble, Squeak, and my favourite – 'Egg On' – short for "egg on toast". He was a black-and-white Dutch rabbit, and there was another ginger-and-white one I called Honey. With each new litter,

Father would build another level to the hutch tower, making room for more.

I now understand, those hutches weren't just a place for the rabbits. They were bait. He built them layer by layer, drawing me in while he worked, always keeping watch, always making sure no one else could see. From there, with the entire garden in his view, he could keep watch for anyone approaching and stop his evil act if necessary. He was cunning; sly like a fox.

Animals filled our garden, each one an attempt at companionship in a house where safety was never certain. But they never lasted long. My hamster lived on top of those hutches, tucked away in its own cage. Everything was fine until the rats showed up. I remember seeing one run across the bottom of the garden by the shed one morning, and not long after, I found my hamster with its nose bitten, courtesy of one of the rats. That marked the end of the rabbits and hamsters. My brother, however, kept his hamster inside the house, often slipping it into his top pocket and forgetting to put it back in its cage. One night, in the dim light of the bedroom, Mum felt something run across the bottom of her bed. Thinking it was a rat, she kicked off the blankets in a panic. Unfortunately, the hamster didn't survive.

In our garden, there were three types of apple trees: two for cooking and one for eating. The little eating apple tree was where the tortoises lived, their small houses tucked beneath its branches. There were also two pear trees: Conference and Williams. The Williams pears needed to be ripened in the shed before we could eat them, but the Conference pears were ready to eat right off the tree after a quick rinse.

Mum's garden was her refuge, a place where she could disappear for hours, away from the noise and demands of the house. And I followed her like a shadow, seeking comfort, safety, and maybe a little piece of that quiet world she created out there.

CHAPTER FIVE

Home Discomforts

As I open the porch door, the empty shelves on the right come into view, some at eye level and others higher up. It's a small porch, but Mum always managed to cram as many of her potted geraniums as possible onto those shelves during the winter. Even though it was now summer, that musky, earthy smell still lingered in the air, familiar.

I turn to my left and spot it, a tiny lip on a small panel of the wall. You wouldn't notice it unless you knew it was there. He had created a secret panel. As I pull at the lip, the panel folds down, revealing a spare door key hanging neatly on a little hook.

For most people, home is a safe haven, a place to relax and let the world pass you by. A sanctuary where you feel safe, surrounded by people who love you and are supposed to protect you at all costs. A retreat where warmth, love, laughter, and the smell of good food fill the air. A comfy bed to lay your head, away from the madness of the outside world, the cold, the wet, the fast cars, the scary dark alleyways, and all those strange people. The kind of place where strangers are the danger. No one had ever said anything about fathers.

As I slide the key into the door, I know exactly where I'd rather be, and it isn't here. The outside world, as unpredictable as it might be, feels far less intimidating than the one I'm about to step into. Out there, I know where I stand. In here, nothing feels certain.

Once through the second door, I walk briskly down the hallway, casting a quick glance at the staircase on my right. The faster I pass it, the less chance there is of him appearing at the top, beckoning me to join him.

It would not be uncommon for him to do this. He didn't concern himself with taking risks; in fact, it seemed to add to his entertainment. If he thought Mum would be in the kitchen long enough, it was just enough time for him to make me jerk him off!

Today I'm lucky; he's not there. I approach the entrance to the living room and as my eyes skate quickly around the room, again I do not see him. I sigh a sense of relief. He would not physically abuse me there, but any moment left alone with him could give him a chance to make inappropriate gestures or even tell me what he had lined up for me on our next encounter. Being alone with him was never a good thing.

I begin to relax as the smell of Mum's cooking takes over, guiding me towards the kitchen. As I step inside, I see her. Mum is busy at the counter, apron strings tied neatly, her movements calm and familiar. The sight of her steadies me. I attach myself to her presence like a magnet to a fridge door, finally able to let my guard down just a little.

"Mum, can I have something to eat?" I ask, my appetite suddenly kicking in.

She opens one of the kitchen cupboards and hands me two rich tea biscuits. My eyes flicker to another cupboard, the one where she keeps the chocolate biscuits for herself, but I know better than to ask. Instead, I spread a bit of margarine on the plain ones, pretending it's the same. I sit at the kitchen table on the swivel chair. It's fun for a child to go round and round on one of those chairs, kicking off the wall to get more movement, but my added advantage is that by swinging round, it gives me a 360-degree view of where he could be coming from. After all, he could come from the garage door, which was behind me, or from the shed down the garden in front of me.

And then I see him.

Today it is the garden shed. Wearing worn, paint-covered jeans and no top on this hot day, he wears a posture that shouts he is very full and sure of himself. To me, he is pure cringey. The garden is 100 feet long, and I hate watching him take every step that draws him nearer to us.

The stench of body odour interrupts the aroma of Mum's dinner. "Go get cleaned up," she tells him. "Dinner won't be long." So far, it hasn't been a bad day. I haven't had to look at him for long, and better still, Mum says she doesn't have to work tonight. An instant weight lifts from my shoulders.

After dinner, still clinging to Mum, we move to the living room to watch telly. A few soap operas later, it's bedtime. As I get up from the floor where I've been glued to Mum's ankle, all I can think is, *Get this over with quickly.* The nightly routine of kissing Father goodnight on the cheek fills me with dread. I take a sliver of comfort from knowing I haven't got to kiss him on the lips. Even still, I am revolted by the mere idea of even being near him.

Being closest to Mum, I lean over and kiss her first, then move towards him. Eeek! Going upstairs, I wipe my mouth as if to erase any contact.

Upstairs, I change into my nightclothes behind the bathroom door, brush my teeth, and climb into bed. In the dark, I create the safe place in my mind that I've been building for as long as I can remember. I do my hardest to create nice thoughts in my head. From a very early age, I created a safe illusion to make myself feel secure. In the illusion, I'm all tucked up in a pram; the blankets are tucked in tight, all the weatherproof covers are over the pram, and it's pouring with rain, yet the pram is secure, dry, and a safe place to be. There is a strong protective figure holding tight to the pram handle and keeping me safe from the storm. To this day, I cannot sleep without a small light on.

Coming back to reality, I drift off to sleep. In the middle of the night, I am startled, woken by a hand touching me between my legs. I really don't want this; I just want to sleep. I have no choice; Father persists. Eventually, his penis is in my mouth – again – and when he is finished, I quietly sob myself to sleep. My sister is in the same room, and she sleeps through it all. I often think I should have bitten into that disgusting "thing" and watched my father try and explain that one away!

CHAPTER SIX

School

Now, life at home was one thing: Mum in the garden, me following her around, and Father busy with his makeshift projects – but school, that was a different world entirely. Crossing the main road with Mum, it was like stepping into another universe, leaving behind the safety of the garden and the tortoises and walking into something much bigger, much grander.

The gates of the school loomed ahead of us, tall and imposing, and I remember feeling both excitement and a hint of unease. Beyond those gates, the path stretched out in front of me, seemingly endless. On the left was a vast field, rolling out as far as my eyes could see, and to the right, an enormous building, towering over everything. With Mum's hand in mine, we walked for ages alongside side that building – a building that showed no signs of coming to an end. Its Georgian windows stared down at me like eyes all the way, and the stone walls seemed to whisper old stories. If I'd known about Harry Potter back then, I'd have sworn I was walking in the grounds of Hogwarts itself. This, however, was the start of my own adventure.

When we finally reached the end of it, another identical building came into view right beside it. Like two giants, standing side by side, with nothing but a pair of playgrounds separating them. The first playground was for the senior girls, and the second one was for us, the infants. We walked

30

past the first, then cut across the second, until we reached the steps that led up to the entrance of my new school. We climbed them together, my little hand still clinging to Mum's. A left turn, then another left, and we were at my classroom. It was now my time to step into a new chapter.

Inside, we were greeted by the echoes of shuffling little feet and the muffled hum of distant laughter. The smell of chalk dust and floor polish filled the air, mixing with the faint scent of children's lunches tucked into brown paper bags.

Mum dropped me off in front of the sandpit without a fuss. "Play here," she said, as if giving instructions to a stranger. Her words were as quick as her exit, her figure disappearing from the room, down the path, without a backward glance. That was Mum; here, then gone, her presence like a whisper that faded before you could grasp it. I stood alone, unsure, waiting for something or someone to tell me what to do next. I didn't feel sad to see her leave. I wasn't used to much attention at home from Mum, so there wasn't much to miss. A hug, a cuddle, concern never existed.

Once Mum had gone, I started to take in more of my surroundings. The school felt old, like it had been there for centuries. I remember walking just beyond the classroom and turning left, to be greeted by a never-ending corridor lined with metal pegs for coats and homemade PE bags. Just the interval of a classroom door sat in between and then the pattern repeated itself, as far as the eye could see. Dust and something ancient seemed to fill the air. Each classroom door was solid wood, heavy with square glass panes at the top, and they had big, round, white knobs. When those doors opened or closed, the clunk echoed all the way down that corridor, just like the sound of the school bell. There was no escaping that bell; its ring seemed to shake the walls. Whether I was happy to hear it depended entirely on what it meant. Playtime? Wonderful. Home time? Not so impressed.

Before playtime, we had milk time. Mum had milk delivered at home; I can still see her sipping the cream that sat at the top of every bottle before it even got to the fridge, but these bottles were miniature, the cutest little versions, with tiny straws for us to sip from. There used to be an advert on the telly about milk, featuring these stripey straws that would swoop in and drink your milk if you didn't finish it quickly enough. The straw was called Humphrey, and it came with a little jingle: *"Watch out, watch out, there's a Humphrey about!"* Somehow, I remember those words being chanted at me as we sat around the tables, everyone gulping down their milk before being let loose into the playground.

If you were lucky, it might be your turn to play on Sammy the Steam Engine, a massive metal train in the playground, standing proudly like a monument to childhood adventures. The chosen few wore colourful bands across their chests, marking it as their turn to climb, explore, and let their imaginations run wild. I remember falling a few times in that playground; scraped knees and tears were just part of the experience, but the thrill of the playground always outweighed the bumps and bruises.

I distinctly remember one day, as I was playing on the playground, a senior girl from the adjacent playground barrelled into me, knocking me flying to the ground. Either she or I had crossed the visible dividing line. The sharp sting shot through my hip, and I felt my knee scrape against the rough concrete. I waited, half-hoping someone would come to help, but no one even glanced my way. I brushed myself off, clenching my jaw to keep from crying as I limped off, my hip throbbing with every step. The stinging ache was more than physical; it was a reminder, as harsh as Mum's indifference, that my pain was mine to carry.

Lunchtimes were just as memorable. We lined up in neat rows, like little soldiers, marching down the long path back to the big gates where Mum had first brought me in. The dining hall served children from both of those giant buildings; it must have been a military operation, planned with precision, to make it work as well as it did. I always looked forward to the half-coated biscuits that sometimes came with dessert. One of my clearest memories is of a competition at the dinner table, trying to see who could make their face go the reddest by holding their breath. It's a wonder we didn't burst a blood vessel all in the name of fun.

I was happy enough at school, though I didn't excel in much. My mind was always elsewhere, caught up in the constant worry of what I'd be returning home to. That nagging fear always hovered in the background, never letting me fully focus on the here and now.

Junior school was on the upper level of the infants, but their playground was further up the path, on the far side of the second building. It felt like a step up, a place where I could start to carve out a bit of independence. I found a love for netball there, and any excuse to stay at school longer was welcomed. It was a chance to stay out of the house a little later, to avoid whatever waited for me back home. Once a year, a farm would visit the school, bringing with it animals that I adored. I looked forward to that day more than anything.

At the far end of the junior school corridor, there was a dark, winding staircase. It always felt out of place, like something from another time. Word had it that the staircase was haunted, and none of us dared to go near it. We'd whisper about it in hushed tones, daring each other to take a step closer, but we never did. It was just one of many mysteries in a place full of them, where the boundaries between the real and the imagined seemed to blur as easily as the ringing of the school bell that echoed through those never-ending halls.

School was its own little world, separate from the home and garden I knew, and those days spent in the playground or the classroom were moments of escape, a brief respite from the life waiting on the other side of the road.

When I reached puberty and my bust started to form, all I wanted to do was flatten my breasts in any way I could. I didn't want to be even more sexually attractive to him. I'd put layers upon layers of jumpers on. I can still remember Mum's amusement as she'd recount to anyone who'd listen how I'd dramatically declared my wish to "cut them off". It never occurred to her to be alarmed by such a statement and caringly ask, "Why would you even say something like that?" Caring wasn't in her vocabulary.

CHAPTER SEVEN

Fragments of Us

I always knew Mum had met Father through her best friend at school, but it wasn't until recently that I came to learn their friendship went back even further, starting in primary school. That best friend was Rose, my father's favourite sister. It's funny to think that such a small connection, a schoolgirl friendship, could set in motion the life I was born into; a life that unfolded with all of these layers of love, resentment, secrets and twists and turns.

Mum never hesitated to remind me that I was not planned. She didn't want me, and she didn't make any bones about it. She never shied away from letting me know "I was an accident"; she'd say it with a shrug, her voice always matter-of-fact. There was even another baby after me, a little girl she lost through miscarriage, and I couldn't help but wonder, growing up, if things would have been different if she had survived. Would it have been her it happened to, instead of me? Would she have been the daughter Mum wanted? Would her name, Sally, have meant a different kind of love, a kind of love I never seemed to receive? Those thoughts would creep in, especially around the time of my birthday. While other kids got parties with cakes and balloons, Mum would always brush it off. "Too close to Christmas for all that," she'd say, waving her hand dismissively, as if the idea of celebrating my life was more of a burden than a joy.

Mum, known to everyone as Jo, was the youngest of four. She was born Iris Joan Ivy Darvel, but she loathed the name Iris. The way she'd wrinkle her nose when anyone dared use it made sure no one called her that. She insisted on Jo, a name that fit her rebellious spirit. By twelve, she was already smoking, as a teenager sneaking into the house at night, tiptoeing through Nan and Granddad's bedroom to get to hers. She would tell this story with a half-smirk, her eyes gleaming with mischief as she remembered how clever she thought she was, slipping past them without a sound, cigarette smoke still clinging to her clothes.

My father's family was a world away from Mum's. He was one of nine, a sprawling brood that I struggled to keep track of. His mother was the kind of woman you didn't cross, the kind they said "ruled the roost with a rod of iron". I never met my grandfather. By the time I came along, he was long gone, just a name in family conversations that didn't linger. Jack, the eldest brother, died young, leaving behind only a vague story too. But Ernie, another brother I knew well, was married to Flo, and they had one daughter called Lily.

Uncle Ernie was the stocky one, solid and unremarkable in a comforting way. His personality didn't exactly jump out, but there was nothing to dislike about him either. He took me on my first holiday abroad, and I was bridesmaid at his daughter Lily's wedding. I still cringe at the memory of the horrendous red bridesmaid dress they made me wear; Arsenal supporters, every one of them.

And then there was Aunt Flo. She looked like she would snap in half if you so much as looked at her. With a refusal to eat anything remotely indulgent, Uncle Ernie – bless him

– had to make his own bread pudding because she wouldn't go near anything that might hold an ounce of fat, let alone touch it. They lived in a concrete council maisonette in Highbury, London. As a child, I couldn't imagine living without a garden. What stood out to me, though, was the tall and foreboding rubbish chutes and the thought of how horrendously smelly they must be.

My parents, of course, loved to point out how Ernie and Flo were "wasting money" on rent. "Dead money", my father would call it, telling them they should buy a house like he had. But Ernie and Flo were more interested in their holidays abroad, something Mum never approved of, which meant we never travelled beyond our local stretch of the world. But despite the disapproving looks and lectures, Ernie and Flo were kind to me in a way that soothed the raw edges left by my own parents.

I can still see them, sitting at the dining room table, playing cards in the evening, the soft shuffle of the deck between hands, filling the air along with the thick fog of cigarette smoke. Flo smoked, heavily, like Mum, and between them it's a wonder we could see anything in that room. As I previously mentioned, and I don't know why this is so burned into my memory, I have the snapshot recollection of everyone in the room focused on the telly watching the moon landing together, me on the couch and Cindy at the corner of my eye sneaking off with cakes from the tea trolley. My small world collided with history, and somehow that night still holds warmth.

The memories blur with time, and I can't hold on to all the details, but the feeling remains: Ernie and Flo were a balm, a soft light against the harsher edges of my parents' world. I think of them, and it's like I'm watching an old film reel, the images flickering, but the warmth still seeping through.

Then there was Betty, my father's eldest sister, a quiet, petite figure who seemed to hover in the background of family life. She never married, as far as I know, but she had Sandra, her daughter, and lived with my grandmother, I'm guessing, for her entire life. I don't remember much about Betty, apart from that she looked nothing like her sisters. She was always there, a constant presence and companion for my grandmother.

Brenna, the youngest sister, the baby of the family, married Alex. They had Jules and a son whose name slipped from my memory over the years. Brenna and Alex lived close to my Aunt Rose and Uncle Don, but despite the proximity, we never saw much of them. Mum once told us why they didn't keep in touch, but the reason faded from my mind.

There was another sister, Joan, who floated somewhere on the periphery of family gatherings. I never saw much of her either, and she remains a vague figure in my memories.

Then there was Les, who I believe was the youngest brother in the family. He was the one who most resembled my father in looks, but unlike him, Les was a drinker. After the war, he and his wife, Lil, settled in Basildon and went on to have four children.

I remember visiting them occasionally as a child, though not as often as my Aunt Flo and Uncle Bob, who lived just down the road. In the end, Aunt Lil left Les, and quite a few years later, he passed away from throat cancer.

From time to time, I've seen my cousins around Basildon, but I've always been reluctant to engage with them because of the secret I've carried.

Then there was Flo and Bob. We were close to them. Flo, another of my father's sisters, got on well with Mum and Father. Flo was an outspoken, no-nonsense kind of woman who probably took after her mother. I remember her sharp remarks and sternness often bringing a wry smile to my face. She never directed it at me, so I found her toughness oddly comforting.

Uncle Bob was my favourite. He had a way with kids, always playful and fun. As a small child, I can still remember him bouncing me on his knee, singing, "Nick, nack, paddy whack, give the dog a bone." He was the kind of uncle who made you feel seen. My first memory of Basildon involves him. One night, in what felt like the dead of night, I was pulled from my bed, groggy and confused. Uncle Bob had had a heart attack, and Mum and Father rushed to help. I remember the drive to Basildon Hospital, the way the swimming pool on the corner always signalled we had arrived. For some reason, in the hospital lift, I worked out that the building must have been built on a hill because we went in on one floor, went down in the lift, and still came out on the same level. Strange, the things a child notices.

Uncle Bob went on to have a heart bypass. I'd never heard of such a thing back then, but it kept him going for another 22 years. His eldest son, Teddy, was the quiet one, while Jerry, the other son, was lively and chatty. We always got along well. In later years, they had a Great Dane named Blue, a massive dog who liked to steal women's handbags.

No one dared to chase him; his size made sure of that, and it became a bit of a running joke.

Then there was Rose, my father's favourite sister. She and Uncle Don lived in Islington, London, with their four children, Richard, the eldest, followed by Sarah, Grace and Rachel. Rose had a warmth about her that I liked. She was deeply religious, something that didn't quite gel with me, my parents' opinions rubbing off on me, but her kindness made up for it.

Uncle Don had an electrical shop, and my Uncle Alex worked there with him for years, if I remember correctly. My most vivid memory of Rose and Don's home was one winter's evening when heavy snow fell. The street seemed to glisten in the light of the snow, and us kids couldn't resist playing outside, the cold night lit up like a magical playground. We ran up to the park at the top of their road, bundled in coats and scarves, having the time of our lives.

Their home was warm and inviting, full of character, traits I've tried to recreate in my own home. They had a back room that opened onto what seemed like an endless garden, neat and perfectly kept. In the summer, that room would be in constant use. The front room was where the fire would be glowing, and after playing in the snow, we'd return there, homemade cakes and hot drinks waiting for us.

When video recorders were first released, Uncle Don, being in the electrical business, seemed to be the first person to own one. I still remember the excitement that came with it. Out of all their children, it was Sarah and Grace I connected with the most. We were around the same age, but they were as different as night and day. Sarah was talkative and full of life, while Grace was quiet, almost delicate in nature.

Their home, like their presence in my life, was warm, filled with laughter, and had an unspoken sense of comfort.

Mother's family was woven into the fabric of our lives: holidays, Christmases, all the traditions. Nan lived in Finsbury Park, so visiting her was a weekly ritual, while Mum's sisters, one in Woking and the other in Maidenhead, were part of our holiday rounds. Those visits were part of the rhythm of our year, familiar and expected, especially during the holidays when we'd make up for lost time with big family gatherings.

Christmas was my refuge. The only time I felt remotely safe was during the Christmas period, when the battles of everyday life seemed to pause, just as my parents would recount how "in the war, everyone stopped fighting on Christmas Day". For me, those days were a ceasefire from the fight to keep *him* at bay.

I loved being around my aunts, uncles, and cousins, not just because they offered a reprieve from Father, but because they were genuinely wonderful to be with. My mum had two sisters and a brother, and the three sisters took turns hosting Christmas each year. Mum's elder sister, Bet, was my favourite. She and her husband Tom lived in a big house in Woking with their five children, a small miracle, as their first child was adopted when they thought they couldn't conceive. Then, as life often surprises, four more followed.

Their home was warm and bustling, the walls adorned with portraits of the family they thought they might never have. Out back, they kept an allotment running the width of the garden, just like their parents had. Their house backed onto fields, and I used to think it must have been pure heaven to wake up and look out of the window to see horses grazing in the field beyond. My imagination would run wild, picturing myself living there and even owning one of those horses.

I've always had a deep passion for horses, but now I resign myself to the thought: *that will happen in my next life.*

Bet was resourceful, the best cook of all the sisters, and she had a knack for turning scraps into treasures. Eggshells became food for the tortoise, and empty Oxo boxes were repurposed as Christmas tree ornaments. After she cooked the turkey, Uncle Tom could always be found chewing on the giblets, a sight as traditional as the decorations.

Christmases followed a predictable rhythm. The men disappeared to the pub while we children were left to our own devices. We'd run outside to explore, always ending up at the duck pond at the end of the road. It was idyllic, almost magical. When the men returned from the pub, it was time for presents.

Our grandparents made no effort to hide who was their favourite grandchild; my brother. His gifts always stood out, and it was obvious to everyone. But the real show was Troy, one of my cousins, who tore into his presents with such a frenzy that he had everyone in fits of laughter.

Still, Christmas didn't always come without its tensions. For three years, Mother and Granddad weren't speaking. My parents believed he was interfering in the way they were raising my brother Terrance, and neither side was willing to back down. I remember the absence keenly, not just because of the rift itself, but because it disrupted my sense of safety at Christmas. I didn't like the change, the unspoken tension that lingered even after my mother's sister, June, finally convinced them to start talking again.

Back at Bet's, the kitchen never seemed to empty. As one meal ended, preparations for the next began. Boxing Day morning was an endless stream of frying eggs for whoever surfaced next, be it from a bed or a patch of floor in the house that was full to the rafters. The pattern repeated: men to the pub, women back to the kitchen, children playing wherever we could.

Evenings brought music. My granddad and Uncle Bill would pull out their accordions, and the children would whirl around the room, dancing to their tunes. Grandad, with his Santa-like belly, somehow always had room for us kids to perch on his lap. He'd rub his rough whiskers against our cheeks, making us giggle. When the accordions took a break, pop music filled the air. My cousin, Larry, and I would spin around the room to *"Long Haired Lover from Liverpool" by* Jimmy Osmond. Little did I know how much significance that song would have to me later in life. Bet, forever the homemaker, went to college for cooking classes, sharing recipes with me when I was older that I still use today. I often wished she had been my mum. She was everything I dreamed of in a mother: natural, loving, and kind. I longed for the life she had, hoping one day to create the same for myself.

Mum's other sister, June, was less fun. June and her husband, Pat, had a crude sense of humour that I could never quite stomach. Their house in Maidenhead, smaller than Bet's, meant we often ended up back at Bet's to finish the evening. June's holiday postcards were always the tacky, cartoonishly rude kind, and her jokes leaned heavily on innuendo. I never saw the humour in it, unlike the adults who roared with laughter at *Carry On* films and *The Benny Hill Show*.

Mum's only brother, Bill, was entirely different. He was the uncle who had joked I looked like a prune when I was born, but I adored him nonetheless. Unmarried and living with Nan and Grandad, Bill worked with Grandad painting signboards, a highly skilled craft. He dabbled in art too, creating swirling, abstract images that everyone proudly displayed in their homes. Bill was the life and soul of every gathering, brimming with clean jokes that were miles apart from June's smut. He was warm, funny, and lovable, the kind of uncle every child wishes for.

I still remember my father asking me once, "How come you can hug Bill but not me?" The answer was simple: Bill was warm, genuine and a safe person, but I didn't have the guts to tell him that.

And then, there was my father. To the world outside our home, he was everything a man should be: hardworking, respected, reliable. People looked up to him, trusted him. They saw him as a man who could be counted on; someone solid. But inside our house, in the spaces where no one could see, he was something else entirely. He moved through the rooms like a shadow, his presence heavy and dark. At night, I'd lie in bed, heart racing, feeling the presence of him even when he wasn't there, waiting for the creak of the floorboards or the click of the door that signalled he was on his way.

It's strange to say, but despite all of the abuse I endured at the hands of my father, he seemed to care about me *more* than Mum did. If something was broken, it was my father who'd fix it. If I fell and scraped my knee, it was my father who'd wipe away my tears. If I felt sick on a car journey, it was him who would tell me to look into the distance or if we were at home, place a cold flannel behind my neck. As a child, it totally confused me. How could the man who caused me so much fear, made me do so many monstrous things, whom I hated so much, also be the one offering comfort? It took years for me to understand that it wasn't care at all; it was control and manipulation. He needed others to believe he was a good father, so no one would ever suspect the truth. And it worked. The outside world saw only what he wanted them to see.

Mum, on the other hand, held the reins when it came to money. She controlled every penny with an iron grip, leaving my father to do cash-in-hand jobs just to have a bit of money to himself. In fact, I think there was a time he considered himself to be the receiver of "pocket money" from my mother. He must have got money from somewhere though. Brand-new cars do not appear under Christmas trees from short change. I remember the time my father wanted a new Mitsubishi TV, one with a remote control, something sleek and modern that he had his heart set on. But Mum, ever the bargain hunter, wouldn't hear of it. So my father lied. "Someone at work is selling one cheap," he told her, lowering his voice as if he were letting her in on a secret. "Only £200 because it's knocked off." Mum, thinking she'd struck a deal, agreed. In reality, he'd paid full price, and that shiny new TV was the first thing in our home that wasn't second-hand, on sale or had a yellow sticker on it, which meant it was from the reduced aisle in the supermarket. Their life together was like that: small lies, quiet deceptions, a constant undercurrent of distrust that bubbled beneath the surface.

Father worked on a building site and I use to pray that he might fall from the scaffolding one day and die. That would have been heaven for me.

For all her control over the money, Mum left me utterly starving for love. I followed her around like a lost puppy, hoping for some scrap of affection, but it rarely came. And then there was my sister, Elaine. To her, I was nothing more than a nuisance, always in the way. She never missed a chance to make fun of me, especially in front of others. I feared her growing up, watching as she adopted my father's mannerisms, the same clipped tone, and the same look that made me feel small. Elaine wasn't the big sister who shielded me from harm. She was one who left me to fend for myself.

Terrance, my brother, was always the quiet one. As a child, he kept to himself, but by the time he was a teenager, things started to change. It became clear that something wasn't right. Father refused to accept it and was constantly on at him, determined to prove there was nothing wrong. The house was full of arguments, and there always seemed to be some kind of tension in the air.

Terrance would often give Mum a hard time during the day, and I'd say things like, "I'm going to tell Father when he gets home." But when Father did come home, I chose to keep quiet. By then everything had calmed down, and I didn't want to stir up more trouble.

When we used to visit Aunt Flo, who had two boys of her own, she used to tell Father, in her stern manner, "Leave that boy alone." But things didn't change or settle. Eventually, Terrance was diagnosed with schizophrenia, and life became even more unpredictable. One minute, he'd be laughing and joking with me, and the next, he'd snap. I never knew what to expect, and it left me constantly on edge, walking on eggshells around him.

I started keeping my distance from Terrance, not because I was angry with him, but because I had to. I already had enough fear to deal with in our house; I couldn't take on any more. Not long after Terrance was diagnosed, he was moved into a care facility, away from our house. Confrontation terrified me, and it was that fear that allowed my father to get away with what he did for so long. I wasn't willing to face it with Terrance, even though I knew it wasn't his fault.

Before my brother was diagnosed, he went to a home down in Canterbury. They told my parents to focus on him and not take us, his sisters, to visit him. I laughed when she said that she was told to focus on him because, from where I was standing back then, we were well in the background. My parents were already totally focused on him!

I never disliked my brother – unlike the other characters in my house. I just had a lot going on. I had more than enough to cope with. I think that's why I blocked so much out. Terrance has always been a big responsibility, and I've never dealt well with it. I've always been overwhelmed by the scale of his problems and the situation.

When Terrance went into a care facility, as much as I felt for him, being alone, I knew he was better off there; at least he wouldn't have to deal with my father's temper anymore. For me, too, it was good to see some of the confrontations go, and I lived in hope that my mother might now see me for a change.

Looking back now, I see how twisted it all was. The lies, the manipulation, the fear that crept into every corner of my life. Mum, my father, Elaine, Terrance, they were all part of a puzzle that never fit together, each piece jagged and sharp, cutting in ways I didn't understand at the time. As a child, I was left trying to make sense of it all, constantly waiting for the love and protection that never came. In the end, I learnt that I had to protect myself because no one else was going to do it for me. So here we are, and why I am telling my story, and soon, you will understand exactly why I am standing up, speaking, and telling the truth about what really went on in that house.

CHAPTER EIGHT

The Mirror of Him

Elaine, my sister.

I sometimes wonder how we grew up under the same roof, shared the same blood, and even the same bedroom, yet turned out so completely different. She was small, compact and dumpy, in a way that made her seem solid and immovable. Not fat, just built like someone you couldn't knock down. She had big boobs and a flat bum, and the kind of demeanour that always seemed to draw attention, whether she wanted it or not. People noticed her, whether it was her sharp tongue or the way she could walk into a room and own it, without even trying. I can still hear her voice slicing through the air, always timed perfectly to get exactly what she wanted. It wasn't just what she said but how she said it, the way she carried herself, like she always knew the score. She never missed a beat or let an opportunity pass her by. While I was the quiet one, blending into the background, Elaine lived under the spotlight, and it suited her just fine. She was sharper, quicker, and always one step ahead of everyone else.

Growing up, I was the one with the personality. At least, that's what my mum's elder sister June threw out one day. "Elaine's the pretty one, and April's the one with the personality." Funny how a throwaway comment can burrow into your brain and fester. It's the kind of thing that sticks. I spent years feeling like the sidekick in my own life, convinced I'd always be the one people remembered for what I said, never for how I looked. And maybe it's because while I struggled with my self-worth, my hair alone was short, thin, and cursed with a widow's peak, while Elaine had hair that was the envy of everyone. Long, thick, and naturally wavy, it fell effortlessly around her shoulders, and even I found myself staring at it sometimes, wondering how two people from the same family could be so different.

Elaine wasn't just aware of her looks; she knew how to use them. Small, mouthy, and unafraid of anything, she bulldozed her way through life. She didn't ask for things; she took them. Elaine was the kind of person who didn't need to shout or fight for attention. It came to her naturally. People were drawn to her, just like they were drawn to our father. She had his same talent for manipulation, that uncanny ability to twist the truth and make it work in her favour. It wasn't a trait I ever admired, though I couldn't help but notice how easily it worked for her.

Sharing a bedroom with Elaine should have brought us closer, but it didn't. If anything, it only made things worse. She had no time for me. She was always in a hurry, always too busy with more important things, while I stayed behind, tidying up the mess she left in her wake. I liked our space neat and orderly, but Elaine? She thrived in chaos. Clothes on the floor, shoes tossed under the bed; it was like she couldn't be bothered to clean up after herself. Life was for living, not mundane chores.

I remember one day, when we were young, back when the house had just one toilet, I was in the middle of using it, and she wasn't prepared to wait. She banged on the door, shouting at me to hurry up, and when I didn't move fast enough for her liking, she marched in, sat on my lap and peed, just like that! Lacking remorse or respect, she just left me to clean myself up. Another time, she walked up to me, smacked me across the arm, and then shouted out, "Mum! April just hit me!" Before I knew what was happening, I had received two clouts, one from her and then one from Mother. The blame always naturally fell my way. I was getting told off for something I hadn't even done. That was Elaine, always one step ahead, always quick to get out of trouble while I took the fall.

There were eight of us neighbourhood kids – a lively gang that filled the street with shouts and laughter. My sister led us like a tiny general, all confidence and charm. She was fearless, hanging on to the back of the ice cream van as it pulled away, trying to pull down on the ice cream lever to get more ice cream while the driver was preoccupied. She would swing the tallest branches just to prove she could. When she swung from the highest branch, she would launch herself into the air. She was bold and free, casting a shadow across the rest of us, and we were happy to stay in its shelter.

I was always a few steps behind, her shadow my place of comfort. She had this way about her, a confidence that drew people in and kept them near. When she spoke, everyone listened, and when she acted, everyone followed. And me? I was the quiet one, the soldier marching in step, careful not to disrupt the harmony she so easily commanded. I didn't know it then, but I was already learning how to disappear within myself, how to stay small, how to keep the peace by making myself invisible.

In our games, she was the queen, and I, the loyal subject. She'd climb the tree and declare herself "ruler of the courtyard", and I'd cheer her on from below, dutifully pushing the cart, pedalling the bike, playing the part she needed me to play. Being her sidekick was easy, expected, and, in a way, comforting. There was safety in my silence, a way to blend in without drawing too much attention. I thought, even then, that as long as I was quiet, as long as I was pleasing, I could make everything around me feel normal.

When I look back now, I see how much I depended on that role. It became my armour, a way to navigate the world by never stepping out of line. As long as I let her shine, I could slip away unnoticed, quietly carving out a space of my own in the background, hoping it would be enough to keep me safe.

But for all her boldness and self-centred ways, there were moments, fleeting moments, when Elaine did something unexpected. One evening, whilst Mum was at work, as the older sister, Elaine couldn't understand why she'd been sent to bed earlier than me. Frustrated, she sat on the stairs, sulking in the shadows. It was there, from that hidden spot, that she witnessed the true horror of the sexual abuse my father forced on me.

I was fourteen when my sister finally saw it happen, and I remember clearly what she witnessed. If that wouldn't scar her mind, I didn't know what could! She'd been sent to bed early, but instead of heading up the stairs, she lingered in the dark. Father didn't know she was there, her small form hunched and silent, half-hidden by the spindles on the staircase. When I saw her the next day, she was unusually quiet, her face pale and closed off.

The next day, while Mum was back at work and I was outside playing, Elaine confronted him. It was a bold move that showed just how fearless she was of him from a young age – perhaps why he chose me as his target instead of her. When I came home that evening, before Mum returned from work, I found my father drunk, looking utterly defeated. He wasn't a drinker by nature, but here he was, slumped in his chair, bottle in hand, his eyes red and hollow, empty in a way that made him seem less human and more shallow.

I believe it was from that day onwards Elaine had him firmly in her grip; she never let him or me forget it. Not long after, she made it very clear to me that she now had the power to do whatever she wanted. Elaine said, "After what he had done, no one could criticise, condemn or frown upon her." She believed that rules didn't apply to her anymore.

The day after that, Mum noticed Elaine seemed upset and asked her what was wrong. Elaine's response was cold and final: "You would be the last person I'd tell." Mum didn't push the matter, and that was the end of it.

But Elaine wasn't done. In the days that followed, she decided to use my sexual abuse as material for a school project. She broadcasted it to the class, as if it were just any normal assignment. To their credit, as a result of Elaine's "presentation", the school reached out to my mother. Mother told me afterwards that when the school called her in, her first thought was that I was either pregnant or on drugs. That was absurd! I had always been the most well-behaved child, giving her no reason to assume the worst. I remember the sting of those words, how they painted me with a layer of grime. I was the obedient one, the one who followed every rule. And yet my mother's first thought was that *I* had done something wrong.

When the school finally told her what Elaine had said had happened, Mum did something she had never done before. She acknowledged some level of responsibility. Mum sat across from the teachers and blurted out, "It's my fault... He's been deprived." The words sounded like ash, but no one corrected her.

"Could you elaborate?" they asked Mum.

"Yes, I can. It's because I've denied him sex for five years."

The teacher's response was disturbingly casual: "Don't blame yourself. These things happen." Her face was unreadable.

And that was the end of it. Mother went home as though nothing had changed.

But everything had changed!

For the first time, I felt the full weight of what he'd done to me. It wasn't something normal, something I had to accept or endure anymore. It was wrong. The realisation was like a thin crack in a wall, one that wouldn't stay hidden for long, even if I was the only one who could see it.

When Mum got home, she wanted to talk, but I didn't. This was one time I didn't want to talk about it – because on just finding out what my father had done was so, so wrong, my world instantly turned into feelings of great shame and embarrassment. At that point, all I wanted to do was to go outside and play with my friends, to act like none of it had happened. Her concern wasn't really about me; it was about making sure I didn't tell anyone in the street. There was even talk of moving house. We must have gone to look at new places because I vividly remember seeing a willow tree for the first time. Funny how it's the small, unexpected details that stay with you.

But Mum wasn't good with change, and once she was certain I wouldn't say a word, we stayed in that same house. The house of horrors. She made it clear to my father that if he ever did anything like that again, she'd leave him. I was desperate for her to keep that promise.

CHAPTER NINE

Not All Heroes Wear Capes

You'd think that would have made Elaine a hero, enlightening the school, and that things would have changed, but they didn't.

It didn't make her a hero, and it didn't make anything better. The sexual abuse didn't stop, and neither did Elaine's life. She went back to her world, and I stayed in mine. Nothing really changed.

That's the thing about Elaine. For all her bravado, all her big talk, she wasn't really there when it counted. She did her part, ticked the box, and moved on. She had a knack for doing just enough and then stepping away before things got too real. That's how it's always been with her.

Growing up alongside Elaine was like waiting for something that never came. I was always trailing in her shadow, hoping, waiting for her to be the big sister I needed. Instead, I became a burden in her eyes, always in the way, always slowing her down. She moved through life with such certainty, like she knew exactly where she was going, and I was just this inconvenient weight she had to drag along. Every time we were with other people, she'd throw me under the bus without hesitation, mocking me with that same smirk, the one that made sure everyone else was laughing at me too. But it wasn't just the teasing; it was deeper than that. There was something about her that made me wary, something sharp beneath the surface.

It hit me as we got older that Elaine was becoming more and more like our father. She had his cold stare, the one that cut right through you and left you feeling like you were less than nothing. She had that same way of speaking too, words like weapons, quick and cutting, meant to hurt. And they did. I felt it every time. I didn't just fear her because of what she said or did; it was who she was becoming. Like our father had left his blueprint behind, and Elaine was following it, step by step, becoming a version of him I couldn't stand to face. She didn't do the terrible same physical things to me as our father, but her words, her looks, the way she could make me feel so small. I kept waiting for her to step in, to protect me, but that moment never came.

Instead, she did the opposite. When everything finally came to light, when the truth about what our father had done could no longer be ignored, I thought maybe – just maybe – Elaine would change. That she'd finally take up the role of protector, be that big sister I'd always imagined she could be. But she didn't. She packed her bags and left. Off to Canada, to stay with Mum's cousin for a month, and thereafter off to wherever she could escape to. She left me there, more alone in that house than ever. She wasn't the one standing up for me. She was the one running away, putting as much distance between herself and the past as she could. Every time she left, every time she found some new place to go, it felt like she was saying, "You deal with it, April. You're on your own."

She was determined to escape and get as far away from the mess as possible, and I was just part of the mess she couldn't wait to shake off. The hurt wasn't just in the leaving; it was in the waiting. I had spent so long waiting for her to protect me, to tell me that everything was going to be alright.

But that never happened. Instead, she mirrored our father in so many ways, and the more I looked, the more I saw him in her. That cold detachment, that ruthless ability to cut ties and not look back, even when it was me, her sister, left behind. I was never her priority. I was always the inconvenience, always in her way, waiting for something that was never going to come.

What hurt most wasn't just the way she left, but the fact that she could leave so easily. No second thoughts, no hesitation. She was gone, and I was left to fend for myself, like I'd always been. The truth is, Elaine never saw herself as my protector, and I spent too many years hoping she would. In the end, all she left me with was the understanding that I was on my own, that I'd always been on my own. And that realisation, that slow, painful truth, was harder to bear than anything she ever said or did.

So here she is. Elaine, my sister. A walking contradiction, so different from me in every possible way, yet tied to me in ways neither of us can escape. For better or worse, she's a huge part of my story, and along with everyone else, I will not let her silence me further.

CHAPTER TEN

Nothing Changed But Me

After the incident at school, my mother gave me instructions that felt both futile and powerful in their simplicity: scream out if he came near me again. And that's exactly what I did. One night, as he crept into the bedroom, I didn't sob quietly into my pillow as I always had before. Instead, I let my voice break the silence, loud and unrelenting. To this day, I can still see them both standing beside my bed, my mother, silent and unreadable; my father, defensive and indignant, claiming it was my brother, not him, who had done the unforgivable.

The next day, the phone rang. It was Father, calling me from work. His voice was unusually soft, almost rehearsed, as he apologised, admitting he understood I could never forgive or forget what he had done. When I hung up, I told my mother what he'd said, expecting, maybe, sympathy, or more importantly, action. But all she said was, "We can forget about it now."

Forget about it? What happened to her promise, her bold assurance, that she would leave him if it ever happened again? Her words echoed, empty, and with them came the realisation that life was full of such empty promises, from both of them. He continued, as ever, over and over.

I was alone now, more than ever, fending off this monster of a father. The sexual abuse had turned into a suffocating kind of psychological warfare. Maybe that's why I couldn't stop wondering, how had my mother not noticed? All those years of him leaving their bed in the middle of the night. How could she not know? Or was she simply turning a blind eye, choosing her peace over my safety?

I even remember Mum catching him hovering at the top of the stairs, looking suspicious. When she confronted him, he just said, "It's my house, and I'll do what I want." That was all. He didn't have to explain himself, and Mum didn't push him any further. She just accepted it, and that was the last time she *ever* questioned him.

I knew better than to challenge him outright. Father when angry – truly angry – was a force that terrified me. And yet, there were moments when I had no choice but to face his wrath. Once I knew it was wrong, the endless times I refused him are etched into my memory like scars. It amazes me now to think I stood my ground. How did I do it? Where did that courage come from?

I can still hear his rage echoing in my ears the night I told Mother that I was too old to kiss him goodnight. He exploded, his fury a storm I couldn't face, and I did what I always did; I ran. I left the house for a while to let the storm pass. Running away was my survival mechanism, my way of handling confrontation. It's strange to think of the rare times I stayed, rooted in place, refusing to back down. What makes one confrontation different from another? I've never quite figured it out. Maybe it's the weight of the moment, that tipping of the scales when something matters just enough to hold your ground. Or maybe it's something else entirely. Who knows? Flight or Freeze comes to mind.

I began to disappear into myself, my life folding in. From then on, knowing fully that it was wrong, trying to avoid Father was second nature, an instinct as necessary as breathing. I developed a sixth sense, a kind of radar finely tuned to his presence. The muffled hum of the television, even the faint scent of his aftershave in the hallway, all became signals, reminders to stay on high alert. I learned his routines as if I were studying for an exam: the times he'd linger in the living room or when he might drift upstairs.

There was a fragile, invisible boundary in every room, a sense of where I could stand, move, or even sit without risking too close an encounter. I'd enter a room only if I was certain he wasn't there, always with an escape route in mind. Sometimes, I'd even catch sight of him from a distance and feel my chest tighten, as if my body knew before my mind did.

When he was near, I'd go silent, almost as if speaking might somehow reveal my presence. I kept conversations short, my answers clipped and cautious. Every word felt like a risk. It became a habit, the quiet art of avoiding him, like navigating an endless maze where the walls shifted with every step, always pushing me towards safety.

The house took on a kind of stillness. Rooms I once felt at ease in became unfamiliar, almost foreign, and every ordinary detail felt charged. The bedroom was the worst place for feelings of tension, a reminder of how close his presence lingered, even through the walls.

Smiling was my new disguise, a habit I perfected in front of the mirror until it felt as routine as brushing my teeth. In photos from those years, you'd see an obedient daughter, eyes wide, face smiling softly, looking as though she hadn't a care in the world. My lips stretched into a polite, practiced smile, a mask to hide the storm brewing beneath. No one questioned it. No one saw the forced cheer, the effort behind the expression, the way I used it to keep questions at bay.

But the routine of avoidance grew deeper roots. I learned to anticipate his footsteps, the way the floorboards groaned beneath his weight, how the air would shift when he entered a room. I found ways to blend into the background, an art form that required quiet, patience, and the slow erasure of my own presence. This was my survival: to exist only on the edges; a faint silhouette.

Even though he would constantly promise to leave me alone, his promises were as worthless as the man himself. No matter what I said or did, he wouldn't keep away. By now, I outright refused to do what he wanted, but that didn't stop him from trying. Night after night, Father would creep into our bedroom, his shadow stretching across the room as he groped at me, his breath reeking of desperation. When Elaine wasn't around, he escalated, leaving porn magazines at the foot of my bed, a sick reminder of his intentions.

I seethed with anger, not just at him, but at Mother, who turned a blind eye to everything, refusing to acknowledge what was right under her nose. I decided one day, enough was enough. Quite calmly – given how I was raging inside – I took a needle from my mother's sewing basket and whilst no one was looking, I opened Father's bedside drawer and saw condoms lying there. To me, they were symbols of his twisted, pathetic attempts to disguise and control his deviance. He didn't need them with me. Thank God he'd never managed to fully violate me.

With a vindictive grin, I began stabbing through the condoms, one by one. If they wanted to ignore what was happening, then I'd give them something they *couldn't* ignore, something they wouldn't want. The thought of him accidentally creating a problem for Mother and himself – that he couldn't wriggle out of – filled me with a dark sense of triumph. Another kid to worry about, so he might leave me the hell alone!

Of course, deep down, I knew the truth: Mother was far too frigid, and those condoms had probably been sitting untouched in that drawer for a decade. But in that moment, it wasn't about logic; it was about reclaiming some of the power he'd stolen from me, forcing them to face the chaos they'd tried so hard to avoid.

CHAPTER ELEVEN

The First Taste of Freedom

The holiday to Tenerife came out of nowhere. One day, Mum and Father told me I was going and that my aunt and uncle would be taking me. I was 15, and while I didn't question why they weren't coming along, I did wonder why they'd decided to send me away now. Looking back, it feels like maybe this was the first time they tried to keep my silence. Maybe they thought a holiday would make me forget; that a bit of sun and distance could cover up what had come to light. At the time, I didn't think too deeply about it, and I was just excited to be going somewhere, anywhere, that wasn't home.

I do, however, remember hearing my father tell his brother, my uncle, to 'watch her; she's all about the boys', making me feel as if they'd branded me with an unseen label, as if that was all I was worth.

Even now, thinking back, that label stings. It was a reminder of how little my parents understood me – how they reduced everything I was feeling, everything I had been through, to something so shallow. It was their way of washing their hands of what had happened to me in that house.

It was my first time away from home, full stop. The house I'd lived in all my life had never really felt safe, but still, it was all I knew. Tenerife felt like an escape. There was something thrilling about the idea of being so far away, on my own, without my parents hovering over me. It was just me, my aunt, and my uncle, and a chance to feel a bit freer for the first time in my life.

I remember getting on the plane, the sound and feeling of the engine roaring up; it gave me my first experience of an adrenaline rush, the same rush I've experienced every time since when going on a plane. The feeling of the seatbelt tight around my waist, my aunt and uncle sat beside me, talking amongst themselves, while I pressed my forehead against the cold window, staring out at the clouds. Everything felt new and different, like I'd stepped out of my life and into a different world.

When we landed in Tenerife, the heat hit me in a way I'd never felt before. The air was thick and heavy, wrapping around me as I stepped off the plane. My aunt and uncle were excited, chatting away about the hotel and all the things we could do, but I was in my own head, taking it all in. The colours were brighter, the sun hotter, the world louder than anything I'd experienced back in England. It was overwhelming in the best way.

We stayed at a place called Ponderosa, a tall, modern hotel that made me feel a little uneasy. I've never liked high-rise buildings, even now, and there was something about being so far off the ground that made me feel a bit exposed. The swimming pool was closed, which seemed like a disappointing start to the holiday, but we found another pool at a hotel nearby. We walked through a little alleyway, down some steps, passed a few shops and then along the main road. The way we crept into that other hotel, across the lobby, directing ourselves straight towards the pool area, made it feel like we were sneaking around, but no one seemed to care. It was as if we belonged there, and that small act of rule-breaking felt oddly satisfying. I soaked up every moment by that pool, letting the water and the sun wash away whatever was waiting for me back home.

The days were long and warm, the sun beating down on my skin until I felt it buzzing. It was my first proper tan, and I remember sitting there, watching my skin darken, feeling proud of it in a strange way. My tan made me look different, like proof that I'd been somewhere and done something.

At night, though, the excitement wore off a bit. Lying in bed in that unfamiliar room, I'd start thinking. I couldn't help but wonder why they'd sent me away – why now? My parents weren't the ones to take big actions without reason. Maybe they thought getting me out of the way for a bit would fix everything. Maybe they thought I'd come back from Tenerife with everything behind me, that the distance and the break would make me forget the things I wasn't supposed to talk about. It was the first time I realised they might be trying to make things go away, to smooth things over without actually dealing with them.

But during the day, it was easy to forget those worries. I let myself enjoy the holiday, which was something I wasn't used to. My aunt and uncle were easy-going, not like my parents. We wandered the narrow streets, with their whitewashed walls and bright flowers spilling from balconies. We ate thick pork chops at dinner, so big they were funny, and we laughed about how ridiculous they looked. I spent hours by the pool, feeling the warmth of the sun and the coolness of the water.

It was my first real taste of freedom. No parents telling me what to do, no reminders of everything I had to carry back home. For the first time in my life, I wasn't looking over my shoulder; I wasn't thinking about what would happen when I got back.

When the trip ended, and we flew back home, the cool air of England hit me like a reminder, pulling me back into reality. Whatever my parents had been trying to do by sending me away, it hadn't worked. I hadn't forgotten. And as much as I'd loved the taste of freedom, I knew it wasn't real, and not the kind that lasted.

Tenerife wasn't just a holiday. It was the first time they tried to keep me silent and the first time I realised that no holiday could make things go away. No amount of sun or distance could fix what was broken back home.

CHAPTER TWELVE

Discus, Distance, and Distractions

Coming back from Tenerife felt like stepping out of a dream and back into the cold, harsh reality of home. But something *had* shifted. I was a tiny bit older, and tanned, and there was this small flicker of confidence that hadn't been there before. The holiday hadn't solved anything at home, but it gave me a glimpse of life outside the house, a life where I wasn't constantly on edge. Maybe that's why, not long after, I found myself throwing all that energy into something new: discus.

I hadn't sought it out myself. The school had gotten me involved in the athletics club. Out of nowhere, a teacher, someone I barely knew, suggested I give it a try. At the time, I didn't think much of it, but later, I couldn't help but wonder if they knew something. Maybe they knew what was happening at home, had heard the whispers that had started to spread after Elaine had told the school what was going on. Maybe this was their way of helping, of giving me something to escape to.

It wasn't glamorous, and it definitely wasn't something I had ever pictured myself doing, but it got me out of the house. Two nights a week and Sunday mornings, I had an excuse to leave. And any excuse at the time was better than nothing. Home was stifling, and discus became my escape. The athletics club was my sanctuary. To get there, I had to walk for miles. To the make the journey shorter, I would cut through the grounds of Claybury mental hospital. On the darkest nights, that held no fear for me. There was something comforting about the rhythm of it, the training, the meets, the competitions. It was ordered and predictable, a contrast to the unpredictable tension at home. But it meant I could be away from the house much more regularly.

I wasn't exactly outstanding at discus, but I wasn't terrible either. Good enough to get noticed, and good enough to feel like I had something that was mine. For the first time, I was part of something that had nothing to do with my family, nothing to do with what had happened. I also represented the school quite a lot in athletics too.

I even competed at Crystal Palace a few times, representing the club, Essex Ladies, and that felt like a small victory. I'd look out at the crowds, throw the discus, and for those brief moments, everything else disappeared. The focus and the physicality gave me a kind of relief I didn't know I needed.

I can't ever recall any of my family coming to support my activities. I can only remember it falling on deaf ears when I'd return home to tell them about it. But it never bothered me. It was all mine. It didn't matter where I came or who came to watch, it was always just about achieving my personal best. As long as I had done that, that was all that mattered.

There was an old bloke who coached us – Mr Charrington was his name. If you could throw something – discus, javelin, or shot putt – then he was your man to push you further. He believed in me as long as I just applied myself a little harder. He was one for soft words and encouragement; after all, his waiting audience was mere teenage girls, but I didn't need that. What I needed was to feel like I could make something of myself, even if it was just for a few hours a week. And for a while, I let myself believe it.

Around that time, I started noticing boys, though not in any serious way. It was like all my other interests back then: casual, on the surface, nothing too deep. A school friend introduced me to a group of lads on motorbikes who hung around on the edge of town, engines revving, jackets smelling of petrol. There was something about them that hinted at freedom, the thrill of the open road. I'd find myself daydreaming about hopping on the back of one of those bikes, feeling the wind in my hair, my arms wrapped around some broad-shouldered, rugged bloke who'd make me feel safe as we sped along. I imagined warm embraces, feeling properly held for the first time. The hugs I'd known had always come with strings attached, tangled up in Father's twisted version of love. What I wanted was simple: to feel close to someone, safe in their arms, maybe even lying next to each other, just feeling that connection in the purest way. Thoughts of sex crept in too; I'm only human, after all. But mostly, it was the warmth and safety I longed for. Deep down, I knew it was just a fantasy.

Then there was this lad I met at an athletics competition. He was fit, good-looking, a runner who could leap over hurdles with ease. I was completely smitten. Before I knew it, I was back at his parents' house while they were away, playing the domestic goddess, cleaning up all the mess he'd made as if it would make him see me as his dream girl. But when I said no to going further in the bedroom, he wasted no time showing me the door. I felt like a lovesick fool, waiting for him under the bridge by the athletics club, hoping he'd turn up, but he never did. That was my first real lesson in 'boys only want one thing'. Truthfully, I was terrified of getting pregnant, and my body insecurities ran deep, thanks to Father's endless erosion of my self-worth. Mission accomplished, as far as he was concerned.

Even though I'd come back from Tenerife with a tan and even though I'd gained a bit more confidence, I still felt disconnected. I'd watch the other girls in school with their boyfriends, the way they seemed so natural around them, and I couldn't relate. There was a wall between me and everyone else, built from years of keeping things inside, of not being able to talk about what really mattered.

So, I went through the motions. I'd hang out with the motorbike boys, but nothing ever came of it. I didn't let it. My body was there, but my mind was always somewhere else, somewhere that felt safe. Despite the new tan, despite my time away, the confidence I had felt in Tenerife only went skin deep.

But throwing discus, that felt different. It wasn't about how I looked or who I was supposed to be. It was about power, about pushing my body to do something physical, something that had nothing to do with my life at home. When I stepped into the throwing circle, it was just me, the discus, and the moment of release as it left my hand and flew through the air. *That* was mine.

CHAPTER THIRTEEN

The Quiet Strength of Us

It's easy to say someone saved your life, but in Jim's case, it's the simple truth. When he walked into mine, I had no idea how desperately I needed him. How the very air I was breathing had been filled with fear and survival instincts for so long that I didn't even know what it felt like to simply live. I was barely holding on, gripping at life with every ounce of strength I had left, and Jim was the thread that kept me tethered to this world. Without him, I've often wondered how much longer I could have endured the suffocating weight of it all.

I met Jim when I was 17 and he was 18. By then, I had already learned – the hard way – that life wasn't a fairy tale. In fact, it was the complete opposite; an ugly story that I couldn't even begin to tell without unravelling. Yet even before I spoke a word about the horrors I had endured at home, Jim seemed to know. Not in the way that most people would have, that awkward hesitation, the fleeting look of pity, but in a way that made me feel, for the first time, truly seen. There was a depth in his eyes, something that told me he understood what it was like to carry a burden too heavy to bear, and I was drawn to him before I even knew why. He had this quiet way of wrapping me up, not in words, but in the safety of his presence. A safety I'd never known before. Suddenly, there was a reason to carry on.

Jim had spotted me long before I ever laid eyes on him. I was playing squash at the local sports centre, the one where his mum worked. He told me later how he used to watch out for me, hoping for another chance encounter, but it never seemed to happen. Fate, however, had other plans. Months later, we crossed paths again at the supermarket where I worked on the tills. I had dyed my hair, secretly, of course, because I wasn't allowed to, and it was an awful shade of orange, the result of too much "sun in" spray and a misguided attempt at using Father's sunlamp to keep the tan and feel better about myself. My face and hair was a shade of orange and I looked ridiculous. I remember feeling mortified, wanting to shrink into the background, terrified of being noticed. But Jim was unfazed by my appearance.

The first time I saw him, he was standing behind the bakery counter, dressed in whites, with a silly trilby hat perched on his head. He was serving a customer, his hands busy behind the glass counter, but even then, through the haze of my self-consciousness, I noticed his dark, shiny hair. I wasn't too sure about the glasses. He looked at me, and I mean, he actually *looked* at me, and something inside me stirred. It wasn't that swooning, love-at-first-sight moment you see in the movies. It was something quieter, more grounded, like recognition. As if we had met before; as if he was supposed to be there, waiting for me to notice him.

I asked him some silly question about salt in the bread, desperate to break the awkward silence between us, and Jim being Jim cracked a joke. I don't even remember what he said, but it made me laugh, and for a split second, the weight I had carried for years lifted. That's what Jim could do; he had a way of making the world lighter, even when everything felt impossibly heavy.

Our first real conversation happened almost by accident. After work one evening, we found ourselves walking in the same direction. I wouldn't say I was nervous, but maybe a little bit unsure of what to say or how to act. We reached the roundabout at Barkingside and in the middle of it stood a massive oak tree, the leaves whispering in the evening breeze. It was under that tree where he'd ask me out. My first instinct was to say "no". The idea of going out with someone, of trying to hide the chaos of my life at home, seemed impossible. "I would if I could, but I can't," I told him, but there was a "yes" hidden somewhere in those words. It wasn't about not wanting to go; it was about what was waiting for me at home, the rules, the fear, the control Father still exerted over me. But Jim didn't push. He smiled, this knowing smile, and said something like, "We'll figure it out."

As we reached the old Fairlop Oak pub, Jim popped inside for a quick drink with his mate, and I carried on home with a spring in my step. I could never have gone home and told my Mum and Father I'd been asked out by a boy, especially not with the way Father was with me. But somehow, I managed to sneak out and meet Jim for our first date, which was a trip to the cinema. The film was *YMCA*. At one point, I finished my milkshake and made a loud slurping noise, absolutely mortified, but Jim just grinned. He had this way of making everything feel okay, no matter how awkward or strange.

I started working in London, and in those days, the city wasn't just bustling streets and bright lights. It was tense.

Bombs were going off; there was always this undercurrent of fear in the air. The city was alive with possibility, but it was also unpredictable. I often felt out of my depth, especially when the trains were disrupted and everything became chaotic.

Jim helped me navigate all of it. He had this way of calming me down when everything felt overwhelming. He'd do the long journey (20 stops on the Central Line to be precise!) to meet me after work and help me find my way through the madness of the city. I was still a country girl at heart, terrified of getting lost or being late. The thought of missing a train or being caught in a crowd panicked me. Jim would take my hand and guide me through the maze of stations, making sure I got home safely. He wasn't showy about it; there were no big declarations, but he made sure I never felt lost.

I remember one evening vividly. We were meant to take the Tube home from Bond Street, but the station was shut because another bomb had gone off, this time in the Wimpy on Oxford Street. It wasn't unusual for Jim and me to pop in there for dinner if we were passing by, but that certainly wasn't happening tonight. As we walked past, we could see all the windows blown in, shattered glass everywhere. A grim reminder of the violence that was always threatening.

People were milling around in confusion, and I was on the verge of panic. But Jim, calm as ever, led me through the streets, finding an alternative route to get us to St James's Park. He took charge in a way that made me feel safe, as if nothing bad could happen as long as he was there.

We never talked about the bombs much, even though they were always in the background. They became the norm, like this low hum of danger that never quite went away. One of the worst was when we heard the bomb go off in Regent's Park, right near the bandstand. Staff from the back of the building had heard a bomb go off in Hyde Park, not long before. The words that stayed with me most were *"nails being targeted at horses"*. A bomb aimed to maim, not just people but also animals. My stomach clenched. For reasons I couldn't yet understand, I seemed to have a stronger love for animals than for people. Animals never judged and they never let you down. People, on the other hand, had been nothing but disappointing. When your own parents have failed you, it's hard to put any faith in human nature.

The scene felt surreal, almost like I was watching it unfold from a distance, even though I was right in the thick of it. Our building sat central to it all, and we were getting information faster than the rest of the city, given that I was working alongside the police. Every update brought more unease, as reports trickled in with disturbing details.

As I listened, I felt a strange blend of anger and helplessness. I couldn't shake the image of those horses, innocent animals caught up in human hatred. I wondered if I'd ever feel differently about people, if I'd ever be able to trust them not to disappoint or destroy. But for now, I kept my focus on the job, each update a reminder of the world I was stepping into, a world where violence could touch even the most innocent lives.

We were sitting in the office, the shockwaves rumbling through the building. Even then, Jim met me after work, reassuring me and steadying me as we navigated the chaotic streets and closed Tube lines yet again. I always felt safe knowing he was there.

We started meeting up regularly after work. We'd wander the streets together, stopping for tea or just walking and talking. He'd listen to me go on about my day, about the little things. He never seemed bored, never interrupted. He just listened in a way that made me feel heard for the first time. I didn't have to pretend with him. I didn't have to put up walls or hide what I was feeling.

Gradually, I realised that Jim wasn't just someone I leaned on in the practical sense, helping me with trains, guiding me through the city, but someone who made me feel emotionally steady. He was the calm I had never had at home. He was the first person who didn't make me feel like I had to be anything other than myself. The first person I was starting to trust.

The more time I spent with Jim, the more I began to imagine a future that wasn't tied to the past. He became my escape, not from the city or from fear, but from the heaviness of home. Home, however, was still a living nightmare. When Father eventually learnt I was going out with Jim, I was given a curfew of 10pm, which he was very strict about. My father, ever the predator, would stay up, with no lights on, lurking in the dark, sitting, waiting for me to come home. With the wall between the hallway and the lounge now knocked down, there was no escape, no way to avoid the living room. He'd sit there, motionless, the shadows swallowing him whole, knowing exactly how to make my skin crawl and frighten me when I stepped through the door.

He was everywhere; a nightmare I couldn't escape. Home was meant to be safe, but it never was, not in childhood, and not as I approached adulthood. No room, no corner, no moment belonged to me. He'd flash me without warning, his grin burned into my memory, a constant reminder that he was always in control.

The bathroom wasn't private. His eye would appear at the keyhole, watching and waiting. Even the ceiling wasn't safe; a hole in the tile gave him a way in, turning my most vulnerable moments into his twisted game.

The house didn't protect me, it trapped me. Every sound, every shadow reminded me I was stuck in a place I couldn't escape.

With Jim, I didn't feel trapped, I felt free. Free to build something entirely new, something of my own. For the first time, the idea didn't terrify me; it filled me with hope. The imaginary illusion in my head that "a knight in shining armour" was truly coming into view now. At last my vision was becoming real.

It wasn't long before I told him about my home life. I had to. I needed him to know the truth of what I had been through, what I was still going through, and what he was letting himself in for. I couldn't keep that part of myself hidden, not from him. Materialistically, my home probably sounded like a palace to him. We had that kind of nice house, the material things, the kind that gave the appearance of stability. But it was all a façade. I described the darkness, the fear, the control, and Jim listened. Really listened. I'll never forget that. He didn't try to fix things, or offer empty platitudes. He just held space for me, for my story, and in that moment, I felt like I wasn't alone for the first time in my life.

Jim's life had been no fairytale either. Born in Liverpool, the second son of Barbara, he grew up far too fast. His mother had a wandering eye, and Jim was caught in the crossfire of her tumultuous relationships. By the time he was 13, he had already decided he needed to make something of himself, to take control of his own future, because no one else was going to do it for him. He moved to London, determined to find work and build a life, and in the process, he learned resilience. He learned what it meant to be strong, not because he wanted to be, but because he had to be. That strength, that quiet determination, was what drew me to him. It was like we were both carrying invisible weights, and somehow, we found a way to carry them together.

I can still picture the first time Jim took me to his so-called home. It was as if I'd walked into a shell of a house, barely any furniture, not a scrap of carpet to soften the floors. The walls seemed to echo with emptiness, and I remember feeling a slight shock at how sparse everything was. Jim watched me carefully, fully expecting me to turn on my heel and leave after seeing it. But I didn't. I stayed.

I can still see him, sitting on the arm of a lone chair, wearing this bright red shirt that seemed almost out of place in such a colourless room. He reached across to the old record player, moved the arm with a flick of his wrist, and the song, 'The Sunshine of Your Smile', began to play. The warmth of the music filled the space, and for a moment, I was familiar with the tune; it was one Granddad and Bill would play on their accordions. This time, there were words to go with the delightful tune. I was distracted from the starkness of his home. It was as if the song pulled me into another world, and suddenly, the emptiness inside didn't seem to matter anymore.

Meeting his mother for the first time was equally unforgettable. There was no small talk, no polite introductions. She looked at me and without hesitation asked if I'd babysit her youngest for the weekend. I was taken aback, but I realised quickly that this was just how things worked in their house; everyone was expected to pitch in, whether you were part of the family or not. In reality, Jim was the only one who did pitch in when it came to putting money in the pot. Jim's mum lived for bingo. It was not uncommon for Jim to pay his keep and then still put his hand in his pocket to put food on the table for himself and the rest of his siblings.

Jim was the only one working in a house of five, a fact that became more and more apparent as I got to know them. His brothers and stepfather were notorious for taking things that didn't belong to them. It didn't matter if it was money, clothes or food; nothing was safe. That was their way of pitching in. They all had sticky fingers, and because of that, there was this constant blame game going on. Whenever something went missing, they each had a perfect alibi, pointing fingers at one another, so nothing was ever resolved.

Jim, understandably fed up with the constant theft, had resorted to putting a lock on his bedroom door just to protect his own belongings. It was his only way to create a sense of security in a house where trust was in short supply. The contrast between his hard-working, responsible nature and the chaos of his home life was shocking to see. And yet, despite everything, there was something about him that made me feel anchored, like he was the calm in my storm.

That first visit was the beginning of my understanding of Jim's world, which was a world so different from my own. It was a place where survival meant escaping into music, into small moments when the sound of a record playing could briefly make things feel a bit less empty.

We both had to navigate our families carefully, tiptoeing around the chaos and dysfunction, but together, it felt easier. Jim had this incredible ability to make me feel wrapped in cotton wool, like nothing could hurt me as long as he was around. It was a safety I had never known, a happiness I had never known. Suddenly, life had meaning, a reason to carry on, and for the first time in years, I could breathe.

Looking back now, it might sound cheesy, but Jim is my hero in every sense of the word. He didn't just walk into my life and change it; he saved it.

CHAPTER FOURTEEN

Wedded to Expectations

Like her parents before her, Elaine's life was crafted to serve Elaine alone. To the outside world, she was all charm and composure, expertly casting herself in the best possible light. But behind closed doors, she ruled with an iron grip. She had Father firmly in her control, and she wasn't about to let that power slip away. She wielded it with ruthless precision, savouring every minute of her reign. The timeline of events became a blur, each one bleeding into the next, but they happened... oh, how they happened.

The first noticeable shift was Elaine's sudden disappearance from everyday life. It was as though she had evaporated into thin air. She offered a simple, detached explanation recently. "After knowing what I knew, I just wanted to get away." That was that. Whatever storm had been stirred up, she had no intention of weathering it with me. Her role in this saga was over, and she was already onto her next chapter.

Elaine's life behind the scenes spiralled in ways I couldn't have even imagined. She plunged headfirst into online gambling, racking up debts I didn't even know were possible. I still remember the day I confronted her, my last resort a threat: "If you don't stop this, I'll tell Father." But Elaine didn't flinch. It was like talking to a brick wall. Most children would naturally feel uncomfortable at the thought of disappointing their parents, but not Elaine. She didn't care what they thought, especially him.

While I was drowning in the weight of restrictions and expectations, Elaine was living it up. There were endless photos of her perched on a stall beside the next bar in sunny Spain, her hand wrapped around yet another glass of sangria, always smiling, always carefree. She even went on a month-long trip to Canada, supposedly on her own pennies, though that story never quite added up. It didn't seem to matter to Mum and Father. Elaine always got a free pass.

It was always the same. Elaine had no curfew, no makeup restrictions, no rules. Meanwhile, every move I made was monitored and critiqued. Mother never paused to consider how I was coping with everything that had happened. It shocks me to even write that down.

I felt invisible, overwhelmed by everything. Each day was a struggle against feeling worthless, hopeless, and unsure of myself. I carried a heavy sense of sadness, constantly fighting to find any self-worth. In those moments, I felt completely alone, convinced I had to deal with it all by myself.

Unbeknownst to me, before I met Jim, he was working at that very mental hospital while I was passing through the grounds on the way to discus throwing; our lives almost brushed against one another without either of us knowing. It's funny to think how close we were then, without realising it.

There was one trip Jim and I took to Clacton, staying in a caravan at Jaywick Sands. I was 18 at the time and working. It should have been a break, a slice of freedom, but all I could think about was the return. The thought of going back home sent shivers down my spine, filling me with dread because I knew what awaited me: hell. And I wasn't wrong.

When we got back, Father went apeshit, calling me all the names under the sun, everything from "tart" to "slag" and "slapper". He packed a bag for me and threw it at me. I'll never forget standing in the bingo hall with Jim's mum, clutching that bag, telling Jim how my father had thrown me out. But I had to go back. I couldn't leave my rabbit behind.

Thinking back, that rabbit had arrived as a gift from Father around the same time I told them about Jim. There's a photo somewhere – me holding the rabbit, Jim with his arm around me, and my father hovering in the background like a hawk. It was all a game to him. He gave me the rabbit to guilt me and tie me to him. I see that now. I can still picture the hutch he built, that shiny varnished roof gleaming in the sun, right outside his shed. That monster knew how much I loved animals, and he knew I would not leave without that rabbit.

I had been naive enough to keep a diary back then, writing down every little detail of what Jim and I were up to. And my father, like a predator in the night, would search under my bed, find it, and read through my private thoughts. I still remember the way he'd confront me afterward, the bile in his voice as he said, "How come you can do that with him, but not with me?" The ache in his words wasn't born out of concern, it was jealousy, pure and evil. It was sick, twisted, and yet another reminder of the darkness that tainted every corner of my life at home.

Jim didn't want me going back into that nightmare, but he also knew I couldn't stay with him. Conditions at his home were tough, far from the safe haven I desperately needed. In the end, my father only begrudgingly allowed me back because we told him that Jim's mum had come to Clacton with us. Why we hadn't mentioned that earlier, I can't recall. Somehow, amid all the chaos, it just got overlooked.

Meanwhile, Elaine was off living her best life. She'd found herself a bloke and spent the entire summer in Wales, free as a bird. Mother and Father even drove her all the way there and would travel back to visit them. The sheer hypocrisy was staggering. My parents could bend over backwards for her, but I was the one constantly under scrutiny.

Elaine had plenty of boyfriends along the way. None of them ever seemed to stick around for long. I often wondered if they quickly saw her for what she truly was – selfish to the core. She always managed to put herself first, and somehow, it worked for her.

Later, when Jim and I wanted to live together, it was shunned upon and made painfully clear that I'd have to marry him first. There was no room for discussion; it was marriage or nothing. But when Elaine wanted to move in with a bloke? There wasn't even a second thought. No talk of weddings, no conditions. It was all fine by them.

Of course, later on, I came to realise that their insistence on me marrying wasn't out of concern for me or propriety. It was their way of passing responsibility. Once I was married, I was no longer *their* problem; I was Jim's. They used it as an excuse, a shield for their indifference when we needed help later down the line. In their eyes, once the ring was on my finger, their duty was done.

There were other moments, too, when it seemed Elaine had life handed to her on a silver platter. At the supermarket where Jim and I first met, there were several concessions available. Elaine, always persuasive, convinced our parents to buy one so she could launch a business with a friend. They even risked their own home to support her, as if it were the simplest decision in the world. It baffled me. Elaine wasn't established in any career, and they barely knew her supposed business partner. Mother didn't even like the women. Yet somehow, none of that seemed to matter.

Father, always dutiful, worked tirelessly in the shop alongside Elaine, doing whatever was required of him, building shelves, fixing things, and anything she needed to help the business succeed. Even my mother chipped in, working on the tills as if they were all building some kind of family legacy. But what kind of legacy ends in betrayal? Because once Elaine got the business up and running, she did the unthinkable: she threw my mother out. She treated her own mother like a disposable employee.

I remember the shock of it. The way my stomach twisted in knots, tight with anger and disbelief. How could she do that? How could they let her? And yet they did, standing by as if it were just another day.

That was just the start. Not long after, Elaine did what Elaine does yet again; she bought a flat, took out a mortgage, and didn't even tell our parents. She had no intention of letting them know until it was all sorted. It was only by chance that Mum discovered the paperwork, tucked away in Elaine's drawers. The flat didn't have a proper bedroom, but of course, Father stepped in, as he always did. He was resourceful like that. He discreetly converted the inside of a small wardrobe into a space for a single bunk bed, turning that cramped flat into something Elaine could be proud of. Because it was starting to become abundantly clear already that whatever Elaine wanted, Elaine got.

It just so happened that Jim and I were getting married around that same time. It was really happening, our wedding day. And incredibly, my parents handed us £1,400 to cover everything. We knew it wouldn't be a grand affair, but it was our day, and for a moment, it felt like maybe I mattered too.

Honestly, Gretna Green would have been enough for us. The venue, the dress, the fuss, it didn't matter, as long as we were together. But the truth behind the tight budget? Father didn't like Jim. Not that he was going to like any man that I married. I didn't need to hear Mum confirm it later to know. They didn't think we'd last. Back then, I smiled through their doubts and told them what they wanted to hear, but I understood the truth. It wasn't about Jim's character, it was because he was a blunt northerner who spoke his mind, and they weren't used to someone like him. Despite the tension, I never allowed Jim to confront them, all for my mother's sake.

Everything was in place: the dresses, the flowers, the church, the food. All the pieces lined up like dominoes, ready to topple if one wrong step was made. Jim and I never had a close circle of family and friends around us, but in the name of playing "happy families", being that we had one sister each, I took it upon myself to ask them both to be bridesmaids. There wasn't any excitement about the families coming together; it was more like holding your breath, waiting for the collision. The wedding was at St Francis of Assisi, Barkingside, Ilford, Essex, right opposite the school I attended on the other side of the main road.

Back at Mum's, where I was getting ready, relatives trickled in, stopping to freshen up after their long journeys. I wasn't expecting drama so soon, but as I reached the church, I saw my cousin's fiancée in tears. It turned out we'd chosen the exact same wedding dress! She'd seen me in it when they had dropped in earlier.

Jim and I had moved our wedding forward because we'd managed to get the house earlier than expected. It had caused a problem for her, one I would've had too if we'd stuck to the original date.

As I walked down the aisle, loosely attached to my father's arm, the bile rose in my throat, and my skin crawled at the contact. "This is the last time," I told myself. "The last time you'll ever have to be that close to him."

Each step felt like I was walking through molasses, thick and heavy. His presence, even in that moment, loomed over everything.

The day passed in a blur. There was relief when it was over – more relief than joy. I was too stressed to enjoy it. The idea that both of our families could be under one roof filled me with dread, and the tension clung to me like smoke. The worst? Jim's mum got absolutely smashed. At least someone had the good sense to put her in a taxi and send her home before she caused a scene.

Our wedding night was spent at Elaine's flat. No honeymoon, no fancy hotel, just the two of us, on the floor. We didn't have enough money for much, but with the leftover change, we bought a bed and a hoover. That was our honeymoon: domestic necessities, nothing more. And yet, I was happy. So happy. There was something beautiful about the simplicity of it, the reality of being married, and the option to start a new life. London commuting was a nightmare from our new place, but I didn't care. I loved the routine of married life. I was so proud of my little chore lists, stapled neatly into my diary, ticking off tasks with satisfaction. Jim had his own lists, too – he always had. We worked like a well-oiled machine.

It wasn't about shared hobbies or common interests. No dogs, no sitting together watching the same TV shows. But we thrived in building a home, keeping our heads above water financially, and ensuring that by the time children came, they would be loved, fed, and clothed. Structure and routine are what held us together, maybe because neither of us had it growing up.

What frustrates me now is how we didn't sever ties with my family sooner. But my love for Mum kept me going back, believing, hoping, that one day she'd be the mother I needed. Every other Sunday, we went back for dinner. Mum's meals were always quite decent, but her "gravy", if you could call it that, was a thin, tasteless hot brown water that ruined everything.

I kept going, kept hoping, and kept believing that one day she'd be there for me.

PART TWO

CHAPTER FIFTEEN

First Home, Marriage, and Emma and Louise

In November 1982, Jim and I bought our first home together. We never viewed the house together; in fact, I've picked each of the three houses we have lived in before Jim even saw them. For him, it was simple; if I'd be happy living there, so would he. Once the sale went through, Jim moved in right away. Moving in together before marriage, though, was never an option for me.

We'd only had the keys a day when Father came over and knocked down a wall. His willingness to help surprised and confused me, and part of me wondered if he was trying to make up for all the damage he'd caused me over the years. But the help didn't last. Soon enough, it became clear that he seemed to get more enjoyment from setting Jim up to fail. Jim hadn't wanted his help in the first place and had only accepted it to keep the peace for my sake.

Our new home looked like an empty shell, with construction tools and dust everywhere, but it was ours. I remember that first moment standing inside, just Jim and me. It wasn't much, small and simple, but it was ours; finally, a space that belonged to neither my parents nor his, and soon Jim and I would be there together. That was more important.

The walls were bare, the furniture mismatched, but it felt like a fresh start. We were building something from the ground up, brick by brick. It didn't happen all at once. There were careful savings, long discussions over what to buy next, and endless shopping trips. But with each added addition, whether it was a piece of furniture or a new set of curtains, the place began to feel like a real home.

A few months later, in March 1983, when we got married, it felt like shedding an old skin, leaving behind the version of me that had always been tied to my parents' house, to their rules, and their control. As we said our vows, I could feel the weight lifting off my shoulders. I don't think I fully realised, until that moment, how much I had carried with me all those years. The fear, the nightmare, the loneliness, the pressure of home. And now, with Jim by my side, I finally felt free. It wasn't about running away from the past anymore. It was about moving forward into something new.

Not only were we building a home together, but we were now about to build our lives together slowly and quietly like Jim did everything; no rush, no big show, just steady progress. He made me feel safe, like I could breathe deeply for the first time in a long while. There were no looming shadows, no curfews, and no expectations I had to meet other than our own. For the first time in my life, I felt a sense of calm. I'd never known what that felt like growing up, and it was a grand feeling that brought with it a great sense of peace.

In December 1984, our first daughter, Emma, arrived. I was so young – barely more than a girl myself – and completely unprepared for what lay ahead. The pregnancy had been a dream, everything I'd imagined, a fairy tale, really. I loved watching my belly grow, feeling her tiny movements. Back then, we didn't have the option to know the baby's gender, though I doubt we'd have chosen to. Still, deep down, I had hoped for a boy. Not because I wanted a son more, but somehow, I felt a boy would be safer and less vulnerable in the world. Not that I was about to let any child of ours be looked after by my parents.

The birth, however, was nothing like the pregnancy. I'd imagined it would be hard, but the process felt like nature's cruelty, putting me through so much pain before I could meet my baby. I cursed and swore, sounds I'd never made before tearing from me as the hours dragged on. In the end, they decided to use forceps. "Push with the next contraction," they said, but it felt more like they just yanked her out, barely waiting for me to push. I remember the doctors chatting casually about cricket as they stitched me up, as if I wasn't lying there, raw and exhausted.

The moment she was born, though, everything changed. This surge of love washed over me, fierce and protective, a feeling I hadn't expected. But along with it came a crushing sense of responsibility, a weight I hadn't anticipated. It was as if the whole world now rested on my shoulders, all for the sake of this tiny, fragile life in my arms. The weight of motherhood settled on my shoulders like a heavy cloak, and I had to learn how to carry it.

Those early days with Emma were tough. I loved her with every part of my being, but finding any sense of balance felt impossible. My world had shrunk to nappies, feedings, and an endless cycle of exhaustion. I could handle a lot, but no one had warned me just how much a baby could scream. Those cries pierced straight through me. I'd always been maternal by nature, but I'd never been around real babies growing up, and my Tiny Tears doll certainly never made noises like that!

We lived in a three-storey house, and often, Emma would be crying on the top floor while I was on the bottom floor, crying right along with her. Jim and I felt like an old married couple before our time; we'd never had wild nights out, and we'd always worked hard. So when Emma arrived, it wasn't the work of caring for her that wore me down, it was the unrelenting crying and the overwhelming responsibility. I'd find myself wondering, if I were to fall ill, who would look after her?

I managed to breastfeed her for six weeks. I remember feeling utterly defeated when, just as I'd finally begun to get her to sleep through the night, my milk dried up. Living in that tall house, if she didn't manage going through the night, I'd have to drag myself down two flights of stairs for a bottle, an exhausting routine I later faced again with Louise. The love I felt was fierce and unwavering, but those early days were a relentless, humbling initiation into motherhood.

There weren't places like today where you could comfortably feed your baby while out and about. All we had was *Mothercare*, just one in each town if you were lucky. I didn't know how to hold on to the parts of myself that existed before Emma, the parts that weren't just "Mum". It was all-consuming, and sometimes I felt like I was drowning under the weight of it all. But even at my most exhausted, Emma was my world. Every tiny smile, every soft babble, reminded me she was worth every sleepless night.

I'd go into town with her bundled in a sling under my winter coat, where she'd sleep peacefully the whole time. People would lean in, cooing over her, and I'd think to myself, you have no idea what it's like once we're home. As soon as I got through the door, she'd wake, and not even a single cup of tea could be enjoyed in peace. There was no offer of help from my mother or Jim's. We were completely on our own. Back then, there was no time off work for new dads, and I had to face the harsh realities of motherhood by myself. Still, no matter how challenging it got, I clung to Emma. She was my pride and joy, and there was no prouder sight for me than a long line of white Terry nappies hanging on the line.

As for feeding her, it was homemade all the way – roast dinners and whatever else I'd cooked, liquidised and spooned into empty yoghurt pots to freeze for later. This was around the time they started putting safety seals on baby food jars because glass had been found in some. I took no chances.

When I look back now, even something as simple as cooking felt like a revelation. I vividly recall making Jim a roast dinner for the first time. He seemed genuinely baffled, as if I'd placed something magical in front of him. It was a meal he'd never even known existed; his childhood had been filled with tinned meatballs, and on tougher days, he considered himself fortunate just to have any food at all.

In early 1987, I found myself pregnant again, but sadly, I lost the baby in the early stages. I'd been told to wait before trying again, but patience wasn't my strong suit, and that's how I quickly became pregnant with Louise. I'd once sworn I'd never have another baby near Christmas, knowing all the extra work it brought. No way would my children miss out on birthday parties like I had. But here we were, expecting another December arrival.

Everything with Louise was the opposite of my experience with Emma. The pregnancy was tough; I struggled with varicose veins and felt exhausted all the time. But when it came to bringing her into the world, it was somehow easier. You might say it was because I had experience under my belt, but it didn't feel like that at all, especially the morning I was to be induced. I was literally physically being sick with nerves, just at the thought of what I was about to go through. I could barely think straight. Poor Jim nearly passed out watching them break my waters with something that resembled a crochet hook.

From that point on, everything about Louise's arrival felt different. Things calmed down, and then, all of a sudden, with no one else in the room, this powerful urge to push came over me, something I hadn't experienced with Emma. Louise was ready to make her entrance in her own way and in a bit of a hurry! Looking back, I laugh at how both girls' personalities were mirrored in their births: Emma, gentle and pensive, taking her time; Louise, bold and direct, arriving fast and with flair.

A young male student midwife helped me deliver Louise. Believe me, when you're in that kind of pain, you couldn't care less who sees you in such a vulnerable state. But as soon as you regain some dignity, it's another story. Just two weeks later, I bumped into him in our local supermarket, and that was embarrassing!

Both girls weighed exactly the same at birth – 7lb 9oz – but that's where the similarities ended. Emma arrived with a full head of hair, perfectly parted, while Louise was born with a little quiff and a small eczema patch on her cheek that stuck around for her first year. Blue eyes ran strong in our family, so I naturally assumed Louise would have them too. Then one day, I noticed how well her peach-coloured soother suited her and realised why – she'd inherited her dad's beautiful dark brown eyes.

Having Louise was easier in so many ways. By then, I'd adopted a "one day at a time" mindset, convincing myself that if she had a bout of crying, she'd make up for it with a good sleep later. Everything felt calmer. Even though there was more to juggle with two children, I seemed to have this attitude of "no time to stress, just get on with it". Emma became Louise's little entertainer, a luxury that's so hard to manage when you only have one child.

When Louise arrived, her birth was right on top of Emma's birthday, the next day in fact, so Jim and I made sure not to let Emma miss out on her special day. We postponed her fourth birthday party to January 7th, 1988. I remember Jim staying upstairs in the lounge with Louise while the party carried on downstairs, complete with a Humpty Dumpty cake and all the giggles that filled the room.

Guilty as charged, the girls' birthdays were just a day apart, so yes, there were a few joint parties along the way. Quite often, after putting my all into Emma's birthday, I could be found wilting by the time Louise's came around the next day, so joint parties became the better option.

Growing up, I'd always dreamt of having a big family, but life had different plans. There was this programme back then called *2.4 Children*, and suddenly, I found myself wanting to get a boxer dog, something that brought me such joy in childhood. I wanted our girls to know that same kind of pure, unconditional love. That's how Tess came into our lives, a beautiful dark brindle puppy. A lot more work than I anticipated, she became our "point 4" of a child, adding a whole new joy to our little family.

She cost £225, and back then, that was a small fortune. I'll never forget the day after we brought her home; it was like a moment of "what on earth have I done?" Emma, then five, was terrified of her, and two-year-old Louise, toddling around, kept having her little pull-along toys snatched by the playful puppy. Remembering how things had gone with Cindy and my mother's sofa, I knew it was wise to keep Tess outside in a kennel until she matured a bit. After all, we'd worked hard to make our home nice, and we weren't about to let it be torn apart by a boisterous pup. It worked well; whenever we couldn't be with her, that's where she'd go.

Over time, Tess settled in wonderfully, becoming a constant source of entertainment for the girls and me, though Jim preferred to stay in the background. It became a family joke that Tess took Jim's place in the family portrait. She was endlessly patient, letting the children pull her around as Cindy had let me, and soon enough, the tradition of playful, gentle dogs in our family continued. I even started giving Tess her own birthday parties, complete with a "cake" made from dog food, much to the girls' delight.

One memory that always stands out is when our neighbour, Pat, passed a lamb bone over the fence for Tess. Not wanting to seem anything like my mother but always practical with money, I made a lamb stew first and then gave the bone to Tess afterwards. I've always tried to keep that balance. I never wanted to take after my mother in her cruelty, but I did inherit a certain thriftiness. That was one of the few traits worth holding on to.

Every week, I'd buy a whole chicken and stretch it out over three meals. Sunday was roast chicken, Monday turned into chicken risotto, and by Tuesday, it became stew. If Jim was lucky, he'd get a small pork chop towards the end of the week. I'd haul my old women's shopping trolley up the hill, loaded with bargains from the market. Just like my mother had done before me, she would head to Romford market on Saturday afternoons to grab the end-of-day deals on mushrooms and bananas. Saturdays meant mushrooms on toast for tea, and Sundays, without fail, brought banana custard for dessert.

Amidst the hard work, there were many moments of pure joy and chaos. I'd watch Emma and Louise playing together, their laughter filling our home, and in those moments, everything felt right. I didn't have to be perfect; I just had to love and protect them. And that, I knew, I could do.

After what had happened next door to the four innocent children whose mother had killed them, and after telling my parents they wouldn't be looking after the girls, a heaviness settled over me that I couldn't shake. I slipped into a depression that seemed to colour everything. I remember the doctor looking at me thoughtfully, saying, "You're going through a second adolescence because you never really had a first." And maybe he was right. For the first time, I reached for a drink to numb the ache, started smoking, and got a taste for the thrill of going out, losing myself in dark clubs where no one knew me.

Oddly enough, this was when Jim's mum stepped in to help. As long as her cigarettes and bingo were paid for, she didn't mind coming over to watch the girls, as they were a bit older now. We had satellite TV, which she enjoyed, so on the odd night, she'd settle in with her comforts while Jim and I escaped into the night, trying to forget everything for a few hours.

My weight had plummeted; my clothes hung off me, but for the first time, I was experimenting with makeup, dressing up, and feeling something close to freedom in the way people looked at me. Outwardly, it might've seemed like I was finding myself, but underneath, I was crumbling, struggling to keep the pieces together. Those late nights and heavy eyeliner couldn't mask the hollow feeling inside. It was clear that I needed more than just a night out; I needed real help. That's when I was finally referred to a psychiatrist.

I know exactly what broke me. It was the moment my mother first made it clear that she viewed my decision – not to let them look after our girls unsupervised – as a punishment rather than the natural consequence of what my father had done to me. Deep down, maybe I knew she would cling to that excuse forever, and oh boy was I right. I should have followed my instincts.

Jim was out of work for the first time ever, and I'd been doing car boot sales to scrape together enough to buy the girls doll prams for Christmas. Then my mother turned up on my doorstep with £20 in her hand and said, "Take this, but we're not buying you for what he did."

From that day on, it became easier for them to fall back on their excuses. "Now you're married, you're Jim's responsibility," they'd say. They always had an answer, just never the right one.

The girls started to develop their own characters. Emma, quite self-assured and confident, surprised me one day when she was about four years old by taking herself off to the bathroom to be sick. I was taken aback by such a young child not needing her mother's help. Louise, on the other hand, different in so many ways, did not like the word 'No'. My first real insight to this was when she was just 18 months old and had her first tantrum. She held her breath until she couldn't breathe; her lips turned blue, and her eyes started to roll back. I panicked and ran next door to a neighbour, who quickly slapped her face to shock her back into breathing. Thank goodness, it worked!

As the time passed, I did end up taking on several part-time jobs over the years to help make ends meet, each fitting around the girls' schedules. My first was selling Tupperware, then I moved on to the supermarket checkouts. When Louise started school, she struggled with it, so I became a dinner lady to help coax her into going each day. I did cleaning on the side as well, finding ways to keep everything running smoothly while keeping the girls my priority.

It was 1992 when Jim landed a good job, bringing some much-needed stability to our lives. By 1993 Louise was six, and despite all my warnings, she had a habit of climbing the swing frame to chat with the kids next door. No matter how often I told her not to, Louise, as a young child, never listened. One afternoon, I stood just two feet away, with my back to her as she clambered up, when she lost her balance. I turned to see her fall in slow motion, heading towards the ground at such an angle that I fully expected the bone to break through her elbow. I reached out instinctively, but the swing frame was in my way, and all I could do was watch.

Jim was in the shower, but he must have heard the commotion because he was beside us in seconds. We rushed her to A&E, barely speaking, just needing to get Louise there. They operated on her straight away, inserting pins to hold her arm together. I'd always thought it was our three-storey house that kept me on my feet, but those two weeks running around Louise's hospital bed taught me otherwise. She kept me on my toes, in every sense.

Louise had always been squeamish, and despite handling the operation and those pins in her arm like a little trooper, she nearly passed out when the hospital sent the pins home a few weeks later as a keepsake! Another time, I took Emma to have a tooth out and as I was trying to comfort her, Louise's face went pale beside me. Out of sheer worry, she threw up right there, unable to bear seeing her sister in pain. I did not know where to put myself first.

By 1994, Jim had been promoted at work and was set on us moving house. He was right; it wasn't the best area to bring up our girls. Next door, we'd had a murderer; a rapist lived a door further down, and another lad, just a bit further along, had run over an old lady and killed her. The place was hardly family friendly.

It was hard for me to make the change, though. My first thoughts were of the girls, worrying about uprooting them from school and having to settle them somewhere new. But Jim was right. We moved to the better part of town, and now, when you stepped off the train, you were greeted by green bridle paths instead of the concrete sprawl that lay just one stop back, where we'd lived before.

By making the move, we'd left ourselves strapped for cash and hadn't accounted for the car engine blowing up. The one and only time we asked my parents for help, they declined. That was the moment we fully grasped where we stood, and we never asked again.

At first, I secretly wished we could pick up our old house and transplant it here; the new house was smaller, especially the kitchen. I'd grown used to a large open-plan kitchen and dining area, and now I was stuck with a tiny, boxed-in kitchen where I was constantly imagining pushing the walls out. The girls took a while to settle, too. It took them at least three months to feel comfortable in their new school. Even I found it hard to let go, still making the journey back to the old school for my dinner lady job. Eventually, the new school picked up on it and offered me a position, letting me stay close to the girls. I suppose I was clinging to what I knew.

In our new neighbourhood, I made a new friend through the kids and our dog Tess. Her name was Beverly, and she had a passion for home improvements, her biggest accomplishment being curtain-making. I was lucky enough to have her as my own private tutor, and she took me on a journey to make curtains for our little home. I even picked up some bar work at the local social club, a place where Jim and the girls could join me and we could spend time together. Despite that cramped kitchen, I managed to make it look lovely with my new skills. Forever the homemaker, I found ways to make that little house feel like ours.

We've always thought of Emma as the quiet, reserved one, yet she's always been self-assured. Even as a child, she loved nothing more than singing and dancing on stage in front of others. She worked hard at everything she did, always eager to learn from her mistakes, and, most importantly, she's always been kind, finding the good in others.

A sadness quietly entered our home when the time came to say goodbye to our beloved Tess. No pet could ever replace her, but for me, life felt incomplete without an animal companion. Before long, two ducks joined the family, of all creatures! They were possibly the messiest little animals to ever walk the earth, but the girls adored them. Every day after school, they'd change into old clothes just to cuddle and play with their feathery friends. Soon enough, however, my heart began yearning for another dog, and that's when Ellie arrived, a beautiful, light-tan brindle boxer puppy. She had the same spirit and warmth that Cindy and Tess had brought into our lives and quickly found her place in our family.

When Emma was about 13 years old, she came running into the living room one evening, frantic after watching the small TV upstairs. "I'm never going to eat meat again! Have you seen what they do to those poor animals?" she cried. And that was that. Emma, in all her life, has never let a piece of meat pass her lips since that day. Her compassion runs deep, and she's always been someone who listens more than she talks.

Louise's attitude to being told "no" did have its humorous moments. One evening, when she was about nine, she took herself off to her bedroom in a huff. In her haste to throw herself onto the bed, she didn't switch on the light. Little did she know, I'd moved her bed to the other side of the room earlier that day. She went straight to the floor. Oops!

There was obviously much more to Louise than just her tantrums. She was always a good kid on the whole and has a good heart, just like her sister. Unlike Emma, who was more reserved, Louise was the type to hang around with others in the park, which, as a parent, we didn't find ideal. But in reality, it did no harm. She's always been the cheeky one. Emma can have a great sense of humour too when she wants. Louise has always been able to talk for England, but it's never offensive; her charm shines through. She is a good listener too.

Louise has been the sensible one in so many ways. She learnt a lot from both mine and Emma's mistakes over the years. Whether it's been avoiding over-plucking her eyebrows, dyeing her hair, or getting tattoos, she's stayed completely natural. She doesn't even wear make up.

The girls have always gotten along quite well overall, though things were a bit fractious during their teenage years. Louise had a habit of pinching Emma's clothes, or there would be small squabbles: Emma, the tidy one, versus Louise, who, as we used to joke, "could make a mess out of a postage stamp".

As the girls approached their teenage years, I found myself changing in ways I hadn't expected. After years of feeling practically chained to the sink, no dishwasher back then, I started making them do more for themselves. Looking back, I think it paid off. They began cooking, doing their own laundry, and even tackling the food shopping. Anything that eased my load was fair game. By then, I'd taken on what would be my last part-time job: a leader for Weight Watchers.

In later years, I often slipped into that inevitable "in our day" talk with Emma, reminding her of how we never had a dishwasher until she was 18 years old. She'd got one when Emily was just 18 months old. It was hard not to feel a touch of pride at what we managed without. I suppose it will always be a generational thing to say things like that.

In the year 2000, we had our first family holiday abroad. Before that, our getaways were modest, a caravan or chalet in Great Yarmouth if we were lucky. I could be a bit like Mother in my nature, in that I'm not overly fussed about holidays. But unlike Mother, I wouldn't deny my family the chance to experience the world and make treasured memories.

I had always said to my mother that I wouldn't tell the girls about what happened to me until both her and Father had passed. But that wasn't how it worked out. Once the girls learnt to drive, I couldn't risk them visiting my parents and only telling us afterwards. I had to break my silence sooner than planned.

It was Mother's Day, 2009, and we'd taken the girls out for lunch. That's when I decided it was time to tell them about my past. As I spoke, I could see the puzzle pieces finally connecting for them, everything starting to fall into place. They understood at last why they'd never been left alone in a room with him, why their grandparents had never babysat them, why their grandparents had always given their dad the smallest, most minimal of Christmas gifts, and even the hazy memory of their dad having a fight with him. It all came rushing back, and suddenly, everything made sense.

It's funny how, when you grow up knowing no different, you don't question things. But when someone finally explains it, the penny drops. Little question marks had probably already started forming in their minds, especially since they'd met their partners by then and likely found it strange that their other halves had such extensive families compared to us.

I'd assumed Louise, being the nosier of the two, would want to know the full story. But they surprised us. It was as if Emma, doing what big sisters are meant to do, took it all on her shoulders, while Louise wanted to run a hundred miles from it. In later years, though, Louise did come to me and ask for more details.

Through it all, the girls have always put me first. They've made it about *"what you're comfortable with, Mum"*. That thoughtfulness has never wavered. It's always been second nature for me to keep them at a distance from Mother and Father, ensuring they never interacted without me knowing or being present.

In the early years, Mother had a soft spot for Emma. She'd once said herself that she wouldn't repeat history, recalling how her own dad had favoured Terrance, my brother and the first grandchild, over the others. But Mum had never been good at keeping her word. Emma was her first grandchild, and the pattern soon repeated itself. Mum openly made it clear she felt Emma was more like "our side" of the family than Louise ever was. Christ, how wrong she turned out to be.

Neither of the girls were remotely like them.

What I found strange, though, was how Louise seemed to have strong instincts, even before she knew what had happened. She was never keen on visiting, and looking back, it's as if something in her just sensed their vileness. Despite their differences, both the girls grew into incredibly responsible adults with strong morals, principles, and values. We are and have always been extremely proud of them.

While all this was unfolding in our lives, Elaine's life had taken on its own twists and turns. But ever since she found out about what happened to me, I couldn't help but notice how every change seemed to benefit her in some way; whether it was favour or support from our parents, it was always to her advantage, never anyone else's.

Not long after we got married, Elaine decided she wanted to buy a house. I never knew exactly who paid for what, only that my parents later complained they'd lost £32,500 on it. Elaine met a man named Ted and promptly moved into his place in Crouch End, London, leaving my parents to deal with the mess she'd created by renting out the property she'd abandoned. Eventually, my parents had to sell the house because managing it became too much trouble. It was the first time I'd ever heard the term "negative equity".

Around this time, Elaine began showing interest in me for what felt like the first time in her life, and foolishly, I soaked it all up. She was pregnant with her first child and suddenly found my experience useful. She even asked me to be present at the birth, and I agreed, desperately hoping she'd have a daughter so she'd finally understand where I was coming from.

Soon after Sally's birth, builders apparently ran off with Ted's money during a major renovation of their bungalow. Once again, Father stepped in to clear up Elaine's mess. He later told Jim that mother and him had spent £14,500 of their own money to put everything right, with Father working there every day for four months, all unpaid. Strangely enough, around this same period, Elaine managed a trip or two to Disneyworld in Florida when Sally was nearly two years old. I never did find out where she got the money for that, but somehow, she did.

Then Elaine left Ted, and my parents bought a *new* house in Ongar for her to live in, where she paid next to nothing in rent and received endless free babysitting. As for the babysitting, *I warned her,* but she never listened.

Elaine eventually moved in with her "friend", Penny, and Penny's son John, just a couple of miles up the road. Yet another complete refurb was on the cards for Father. It was also around this time that she found out the horrific truth of what the free babysitting of Sally had cost her.

As it was, I only visited that house once, but from past history, I think it fair to say that after the refurbishment here, it was then that Elaine and Penny moved again.

This time to a bungalow, literally round the corner to my parents. It should have been blatantly obvious at this point; Elaine had her eyes on the money.

Elaine had lined Father up for more work, but around that same time he slipped and fell in the garden, breaking his shoulder. He was getting too old and frail to keep up with her endless demands. Somehow, she still managed to rope them into doing little things, though, like dog-sitting when they went away, even leaving her shoes on their doorstep to be polished. I remember how irritated my mother was by it all back then, yet later in life, she conveniently chose to forget.

This was also the same time my mother started pushing me away.

It was at this point that I finally broke away from Elaine. I'd been looking to get a puppy, and Elaine had one she said she didn't want to keep. For days, she allowed me to believe the puppy would be mine, repeatedly saying she just wanted her daughter Sally out of the way before I could collect her. Then, because of a single unsent text message, Elaine decided it was some kind of sign and abruptly changed her mind. My feelings didn't matter to her; all that ever mattered was that Elaine got exactly what she wanted. That was the moment I'd truly had enough, I stopped speaking to her entirely.

Throughout the years, I made it a ritual to visit my mother once a week, devoting an entire day to her while my father was busy working on whichever property Elaine happened to be living in at the time. Our days together often had a rhythm to them: we'd start by strolling through the village, searching for coins, followed by a walk around her garden. Afterwards, I might wash and blow-dry her hair or even tickle her back for her, whatever she fancied that day. Those moments became our little traditions.

CHAPTER SIXTEEN

Driving and Sewing

Before having Louise, there were some liberations where I began to gain a sense of true identity. It was the early years of our marriage, just before Louise was born, when I decided I would learn to drive. I was twenty-five, and for reasons I can't entirely explain, it felt like a test of my independence and my abilities. Truth be told, my family never seemed to believe I'd pass, not alone on the first time. My whole life, they had made me feel useless, worthless and incapable. Why would now be any different? They could never imagine me behind the wheel, capable of taking on the open road with confidence. But I was stubborn and, in a way, eager to prove to them and to myself that I could manage this. One big thing I had going for me was that I thoroughly enjoyed my lessons. It brought on a sense of confidence I had never felt before in my life. From then on, I came to believe that when you enjoy a subject, you will excel in it. A bit like when I learnt to type, I suppose.

On the day of the test, my nerves clung to me in a way they hadn't during any of those lessons. It was a blisteringly hot July day, and I was halfway through my pregnancy with Louise. This time around, as I said, I wasn't carrying as comfortably as I had with Emma and without the air conditioning in that modern, up-to-date car, I wouldn't have stood a chance. The first mistake came as I got in the car; I hadn't shut the door properly. Luckily for me, that one went unnoticed. Then came the three-point turn. I tugged at the handbrake, and it wouldn't budge. I couldn't believe it! For a few harrowing seconds, I panicked inside but managed not to show it; in the end, the examiner had to let it down for me! By the end, I'd convinced myself that I'd failed, no question. Yet, when he told me I'd passed, I felt something shift inside me.

As for the handbrake, the examiner told me I hadn't panicked and had shown "resourcefulness in the process". I was absolutely blown away with happiness.

When I returned home, that slip of paper clutched in my hand, Jim was elated. But when it came to telling my parents and sister, their reaction was abundantly clear – stunned, utter shock. Though I'd always known they doubted me, this was the first time I'd heard it out loud. And perhaps that was what made it so great. For once, I'd surprised them all. For the first time, I felt a sense of control over my life. Driving opened up a freedom I hadn't tasted before, letting me see my world on my own terms.

I remember my first car, a little blue Escort called Miss Ellie. My first solo drive was at dusk, just after putting Emma to bed. I'd never driven alone, let alone in the dark. This was a new experience, and it's common for life's firsts to come with challenges. I fumbled with the headlights, finally figuring them out, and set off down the road, nerves bubbling up as I approached the T-junction at the end of our road.

I've never liked holding people up, and with cars lining up behind me, I felt a mix of pressure and panic. Part of me wanted to switch the engine off and just run home rather than deal with it. It didn't help that my "new" old car had indicators that didn't turn off automatically. It's funny how life has a way of throwing in one more little thing to push you over the edge! But somehow, I managed to pull myself together, navigate the junction, and keep going. It wasn't graceful, but it was a start.

A year later, at twenty-six, I stumbled upon another surprise that would change me. It happened at a cross-stitch party, a quaint little event, like the Tupperware gatherings I used to hold, the kind where everyone laughs and chats over tea. I thought it would be terribly dull. But to my surprise, I found myself drawn to the fabric, to the rhythm of the needle slipping through it, and to the quiet pleasure of creating something from nothing. I fell into sewing. From then on, it became my quiet meditation – my own small sanctuary.

Sewing felt almost magical, like something ancient and comforting, a place where time slowed down and the world's noise faded. It was meditative and therapeutic in a way I couldn't have anticipated, grounding me, especially on difficult days. At three o'clock, most days, no matter the chaos swirling around me, I would sit with my sewing, letting the repetition soothe me. It was as if the whole world could be burning, yet I'd still be there, needle in hand, carrying on. I likened it to the musicians on the Titanic, creating peace even as the ship went down. I might not save the world, but I'd create something beautiful in spite of it all.

The need for tunnel vision feels like a family heirloom, a safety net passed down through the generations. My mother relies on it, just as her mother did before her. My nan, however, was different – a gentle soul with snowy-white hair, sweet and innocent in a way that feels worlds apart from my mother.

Years ago, when I was a child, the entire family, all 21 of us, gathered in Devon for a holiday. We spent a sunny afternoon lounging in a beer garden, unwinding together. As we left, we wandered into a nearby town, and of course, it was clotted cream ice cream all around. The family spread out along the high street, everyone enjoying their treat, when my father decided to perch himself on one of those triangular billboards outside a small shop. The shopkeeper hurried out, asking him to step down. In response, my father smashed his ice cream into the shopkeeper's face, then picked up the billboard and whacked him with it, sparking a full-on brawl.

Unbeknownst to the shopkeeper, our family wasn't one to back down. Relatives swooped in to support my father, while villagers began rallying behind the shopkeeper. The street turned into a mini-war zone. Elaine, always one to find humour in chaos, filmed the scene. Watching the footage later, a few things stood out: the policeman's hat flying off in the scuffle and, best of all, little Nan, blissfully weaving through the crowd, still savouring her ice cream, oblivious to the mayhem around her.

And there it is. Every time I think of something comforting, like sewing, I'm transported back to the people who once brought me comfort, especially my nan. She was an amazing knitter; I can still see her clearly, not just with two knitting needles, but effortlessly juggling five at once to knit socks. In contrast, my mother's first attempt at knitting – a white matinee cardigan intended for baby Emma – turned out large enough to fit a five-year-old!

In 2007, we moved house again and ended up in the house we live in now. The main aim for moving was to give the girls more space. Little did we know they would both be married and moved out after just a couple of years.

Years later, I took professional classes in curtain-making. Even though I'd had my own personal tutor at one point, because I did not keep my hand in, I needed a refresher course. In 2010, I went to college for it, my own little indulgence. I made curtains for our new home one by one, and then there were quilting classes, little hand-sewn mementoes that I would gift the family that felt like a piece of me stitched into their homes. I often thought of my sewing projects as puzzles I could keep, unlike a jigsaw that gets boxed up; each piece I sewed was part of a memory, a story. It was like a gift you could give yourself again and again.

In the quiet of those sewing moments, I was able to reclaim a part of myself, regardless of what the world expected or doubted. Whether anyone else understood it didn't matter, because for me, each stitch was a reminder that I could create my own peace, my own way of putting the world in order.

My mother was furious when she found out I'd told Emma and Louise about the abuse. She responded by doing everything in her power to avoid them, which makes it all the more ironic that she later felt offended at not being invited to their weddings.

Looking back now, it's almost laughable that it took me all these years to connect those two things. It should have been obvious, but at the time I was too busy protecting her.

The following letter, which I wrote to my mother in October 2010, clearly shows how she had already started pushing me away. My reflections are included in brackets; these weren't part of the original letter.

Dear Mum,

I feel I need to write, as I find it difficult to explain myself clearly, without both of us getting upset. I am not comfortable coming over to yours anymore.

*I had not seen you for 6 weeks **(taking into account that I always visited my mum weekly)** and your first words to me were, "It will probably be another 4 weeks before I see you again." After 4 weeks or so, you were then prepared to put me off because of a bit of rain! I then shortened my visiting time to make it easier for you and yet you still cannot commit yourself to seeing me. There are local cafes that can be used for a couple of hours **(referring to Father using them)** and I don't think that is a lot to ask under the circumstances.*

I would like to know more about where I am and what I am doing. Maybe, on a preplanned basis, we can set a date once a month or every 6 weeks, which I feel would suit you more? Whereby I come and pick you up and bring you over here for a few hours? That's if you want to?

This means no one is inconvenienced, which I know will please you, and we can spend some proper time together. Write back or text.

Love from April x

After my mother received this letter and insisted she didn't want to push my father out of his own home, she suggested meeting in Brentwood. Instead, I began picking her up and bringing her to our house for the day before driving her home in the evening. To spare her any discomfort, Emma and Louise stayed away.

Emma and Louise both got married in 2011, and I decided not to invite my family, mainly to protect my mother, yet again. I didn't know how far the word had spread, and we didn't want any confrontations at the girls' weddings.

I had explained all this to Mother, but she stewed on that for 18 months, saying nothing until the day I went to pick her up to bring her over to meet her first great-grandchild. I was so excited at the thought of four generations being together. But as soon as I told her where we were going, she hit me with an "Oi'", the kind that dripped with disapproval.

I was stunned. "What do you mean, 'Oi'?" I asked.

"Well, I wasn't invited to the weddings," she said, as if that explained everything. It was as if she thought my family didn't deserve the honour of her presence now. Who did she think she was, the fucking Queen of Sheba?

I was fuming. I pulled the car over, turned it around, and drove her straight back home. I screamed at her to get out of the car. That was it, the straw that broke the camel's back.

Six letters were exchanged between us, and then nothing.

Looking back, it would not have surprised me if it was all a setup to purposely cut the thread by which we were hanging on, given the secret they were now holding on to about my father's predatory actions upon another family member, whom I did not yet know about. My presence was fraught with danger, and maybe I just fell into their trap.

CHAPTER SEVENTEEN

The Golden Years

Not only had my mother turned her back on me, but also her two granddaughters and their firstborns, all in favour of that fucking monster – my father.

Every day, for what felt like an eternity, I would check the post, hoping against hope that my mother would reply to my last letter, answering the questions I had laid bare. But the postman brought nothing. No letter came. In the end, I had to accept the painful truth: no reply was coming.

And yet, as time passed, something remarkable began to happen. Slowly, like a flower unfolding in the sunlight, my life started to transform in ways I could never have imagined. I had far too much to protect now, too much joy and stability in my world, and I was determined that nothing, absolutely nothing, would spoil it. The strength I gained from the life blossoming around me was undeniable. Jim and the girls would often tell me that I was a much happier, lighter person without the weight of them in my life. For so many years, my birth family had brought me down, but now that chapter had turned a corner.

Emma was settling beautifully into motherhood, a proud mum to her little girl, Emily, born in late September 2012. Louise wasn't far behind her, welcoming her own baby boy, Thomas, by Caesarean late December. If Thomas had been left to his own devices, we were all convinced he would've arrived on Christmas Day!

Emma and Louise lived just a stone's throw away from us and from each other. Since they moved out, we'd managed to find a wonderful balance, spending time together while still enjoying our own lives. With both girls on maternity leave, it quickly became clear that Jim and I would play a significant role in this new generation's lives. From the start, though, we made a promise to ourselves: we would never interfere. We would offer advice when asked, but always with the understanding that they could take it or leave it. We agreed that the only time we would step in uninvited would be if the children were in physical danger and we could prevent it. We also agreed there would be no favourites.

And then there was that magical Christmas morning in 2012. I can still see it so clearly. Two tiny babies, nestled in their car seats under the Christmas tree. It was a sight that needed no words. But even so, I have to say it: they were the most amazing presents anyone could ever wish for.

As winter settled in, it quickly became clear that Emma and Louise had very different approaches to parenting. Watching them navigate this new chapter was fascinating, each with her own style, yet somehow orchestrating their parenting together in a way that worked beautifully. They were learning alongside one another, borrowing ideas and adapting as they went. Though the girls had always got on reasonably well, this shared experience added an extra layer of love and connection between them. It was special to witness, and even more special to be part of.

Winter afternoons often found us gathered in our living room, the fire crackling, as the two sisters shared stories of their first months of motherhood. The babies would nap or feed while Emma and Louise breastfed in tandem, laughing and swapping tales of sleepless nights and tiny milestones. Jim, ever the doting granddad, developed a habit of bringing home a selection of cakes from work, as though we needed any more indulgence on top of the cosy chaos.

In February 2012, we decided to take a family holiday to Tenerife. I'll never forget the sight of the girls plonking the babies down in the airport, both looking as though they'd run a marathon just to get that far. As the flight took off, Emma, usually fearless, went into full panic mode. It was as though the responsibility of looking after her baby at 30,000 feet, without total control, had tipped her into anxiety. The baby, sensing her unease, promptly started being sick everywhere. This was the same Emma who had flown countless times before and had even chosen to jump out of a plane – for fun! But motherhood had changed her in ways none of us could have predicted.

Despite the rocky start, we managed to have some fun on that holiday before a stomach bug took us all down one by one, leaving us bedridden for the last stretch of the trip. It wasn't quite the relaxing break we'd envisioned, but it was certainly memorable.

Back home, life was a whirlwind of baby clothes shopping, lunches out, and endless rounds of soft play sessions to entertain the little ones. When summer arrived, it brought paddling pools and bubbles in the garden, turning every day into an adventure. Our summerhouse, a cosy room tucked away in the garden, was transformed into a playroom for the babies. Every day felt magical, filled with giggles, tickles, and so much love.

The summerhouse became a haven. There were books to read, big bean bags perfect for little ones to sink into, pull-along toys, ride-ons, and of course, playdough, the undisputed favourite. If we didn't fancy tidying up, it was easy enough to shut the door and retreat to a clean house, leaving the mess for another day.

Time, as it often does, began to pick up speed. I was so busy telling the girls that old wives' tale, "Blink and they'll grow up!", that I forgot to heed my own advice. Suddenly, Emily's first birthday was upon us, and I found myself wiping tears from my cheeks, wondering where that year had gone. Then, before we knew it, Thomas turned one as well.

Those early days with the babies were like a dream, a flurry of love, laughter, and the kind of joy that only comes when life feels completely full. The summerhouse stood as proof of those magical times, filled with toys, books, and memories. It was a space where the babies could play to their hearts' content and we could soak in every precious moment, knowing all too well how quickly it would pass.

In 2014, my world shifted quite literally when I developed a back problem that left me unable to do something as simple as placing the dogs' bowls on the floor. It wasn't long before I found myself sitting in front of a surgeon.

"The spongy bit between your lower vertebra has disintegrated," he explained. "We can take bone from your hip and fuse it with nuts and bolts in your spine."

I was horrified. Up until then, I'd always been blessed with good health, and the idea of major surgery filled me with shear dread. Desperate for an alternative, I asked him

121

if there was anything else I could do. "You'll need to go to the gym for the rest of your life to keep your core strong," he said. That was all I needed to hear. I opted for the gym, and from that point on, it became part of my routine, something I had and have to prioritise, no matter what.

Around this time, the girls surprised me when talk of another baby surfaced for both of them. They hadn't found motherhood easy the first time around, but they were both determined to press on. Before long, Louise was expecting again, with Emma not far behind. They'd always seemed destined to do things together.

Louise was the first to deliver this time, welcoming her son Frederick into the world in March 2015, via Caesarean. Emma, who had kept her first birth private with just her husband present, invited me to be part of her second. I stood by her side in July 2015 as her agony subsided, and she was handed her second daughter, Elsie. I was speechless and overwhelmed by the experience, hoping I was more of a help than a hindrance.

If life had felt full-on before, it was nothing compared to now. I can still see Louise carrying her tiny baby while the toddlers dashed around during an Easter egg hunt in our garden. At one point, there were four little ones all under the age of three. Yes, there was chaos, but it was a beautiful, endearing kind of chaos.

Every other Sunday, Jim would be up early, cooking and baking everything from scratch in preparation for family dinner. He preferred to work in the kitchen alone, a quirk I never argued with, as cooking wasn't exactly my passion. While Jim handled the food, I focused on taking the dogs out and getting myself and the house sorted. When dinner was ready, we'd all come up from the summerhouse and gather around the table together, a big, noisy, happy family.

Later that year, another health challenge struck when I developed gallstones. It felt like that old saying: no buses, then two come at once. It was the first time I'd ever been in hospital, apart from having the girls. While I recovered, I used the time to finish the new babies' cross-stitch samplers, finding solace in the quiet craft.

As the children grew, so did our adventures. We ventured to zoos and farms, with Jim teaching them about the organic vegetables he grew in the garden. The sight of the children pulling up carrots alongside Grandad remains one of my fondest memories. Jim has always been the teacher, while I see myself as the entertainer, a role I've embraced wholeheartedly.

I introduced mud pies and slime into the mix, which led to some unintended hilarity when the slime ended up stuck to the ceiling. Determined to make the summerhouse even more special, I decided to paint a mural on the back wall. My artistic skills were far from brilliant, but I wanted it to reflect the joy the grandchildren brought into our lives. I painted a blue sky with a bright yellow sun and green grass running up to the skirting board, and I stencilled the words *"Grandchildren are sunshine to the soul"* across the wall.

I'll never forget sitting with little Thomas one day, pointing out the mural to him. "Look, Thomas," I said, pointing to the blue sky on the wall and then to the sky outside. I showed him the painted sun and then the real sun. Lastly, I pointed to the grass on the mural and then to the real stuff outside. Just as I thought we were done, a little voice piped up. "Where's the writing in the sky, Nanny?" It was a moment I'll always treasure.

The children grew very close to one another, but particularly to those who were the same age. Emma and Louise knew almost instinctively that they couldn't possibly have another child without the other following suit. As it turned out, neither of them planned to expand their families any further.

And so, we settled into a rhythm, one filled with laughter and more love than I could have ever dreamed of. Life wasn't perfect, but it was beautifully ours.

On a shopping trip with Emma and Emily, we stopped in M&S for a cuppa. While Emma went to get the drinks, I took Emily to find a seat. At just two and a half years old, she looked up at me with those big eyes and said, in the most serious little voice, "I'm supposed to be crying now."

"Why is that?" I asked, curious.

"Because Mummy is not here," she replied matter-of-factly.

This was the same child who could sing every word to *Frozen* before she could even properly talk. I couldn't help but chuckle at her self-awareness.

In 2017, another ailment came my way. I was standing by the kettle, waiting for it to boil, when I felt something tear in my knee. I went to the same surgeon who had once offered me that big back operation. After an MRI scan, he explained that I'd need minor surgery and assured me I'd be back on my feet within a few days. But things didn't go quite as planned.

When they opened me up, they discovered the tear was more severe than they'd thought and ended up performing a completely different operation. I was on crutches for 10 weeks and couldn't walk properly for a year. But when those crutches were finally removed, little hands came rushing back to hold mine again. It was a moment of pure love that I'll never forget.

I've always kept a little book to capture the sweet and funny things my grandchildren say. One of Elsie's came just before her fourth birthday. She announced she wanted a vegan birthday cake, explaining it was so that Mummy could have some too. How thoughtful is that?

Frederick, the sensitive soul, gave me a moment of laughter that I still think about. One day, I tried explaining to him that he didn't have to cry if he lost at a game. I barely got the words out before he burst into tears, despite the fact he wasn't even playing a game at the time! Through my laughter, I managed to reassure him with promises of sweets and chocolate for everyone.

As the children grew, so did the love. Every Christmas, Easter, and Halloween was a whirlwind of games, fun, and laughter. We made so many memories, all captured in the countless videos and photos I keep safe.

Then came COVID, knocking the world sideways. I missed my babies so much it hurt. It was during that time I learnt just how much a hug could mean, especially from "my little chicks". When we were finally reunited, there were tears of joy all around, mostly from Nanny. To keep myself sane during those isolating months, I set up a little exercise circuit in the lounge and threw myself into sewing. When face masks were in short supply, I taught myself to make them and handed them out to the elderly people on our street whilst out on dog walks. Their gratitude was deeply humbling.

After years of hard work, Jim retired in December 2021. His first mission in retirement was for us to tackle the renovation of our house. We moved into rented accommodation while the house was extended and transformed. It was a huge project, and I was more than happy to be in charge of the fun parts, planning and choosing materials, while Jim handled the hard stuff. After a year of endless effort, we returned to our beautifully finished home, ready to start a new chapter.

In February 2022, we embarked on a family holiday of a lifetime to Disney World, Florida. Emma had overcome her fear of flying the year before, thanks to her brother-in-law's wedding in Greece, which gave her little choice but to get on a plane. With that hurdle behind her, we finally got the green light for our dream trip. It was everything it's made out to be, magical in every way. We indulged in the magic of Disney, creating memories that were, in a word, phenomenal.

I don't know where the years have gone. The eldest grandchildren will be teenagers next year. They are polite, well-mannered children with strong morals and principles. Loving and kind and we are very proud of all our little brood.

Jim and I feel so privileged to have them so close in our lives. If there is such a thing as karma, we like to think this is ours, a reward for everything we endured in the past. And for that, we are truly grateful.

PART THREE

CHAPTER EIGHTEEN

The Cold Note

My mother's note simply said:

Your father passed away on the 3rd of September, and if you want to make contact, this is my new address.

Mum.

It was straight forward, almost clinical. No warmth, no expression of emotion, just the facts. After eleven years of silence, I wasn't sure what to expect, but it wasn't this. I had imagined so many scenarios over the years; none of them included a note this brief.

I looked at it again, feeling a strange mix of emotions. A part of me wanted to believe this was a gesture, a sign that she had thought of me, that she had taken a step towards reconnecting. But another part of me couldn't shake the sense of distance; the lack of feeling in those words. It wasn't what I had hoped for, but it was something.

I couldn't help but wonder: was this out of a sense of obligation or something more? It wasn't clear, and I wasn't sure how to feel about it. I replied without hesitation, the words flowing almost automatically. I wasn't sure what I wanted to say, but it all came out before I had time to second-guess myself. I began by acknowledging her loss. It felt like the right place to start. I may have hated him, hated what he did to me, but he was still her husband. She had spent her life with him, shared decades of memories with him, and whatever my feelings were, I couldn't ignore that grief must have touched her in some way.

Despite everything he had done, despite the trauma, the darkness, she stayed. I'd spent years trying to understand why. Was it love? Was it duty? Was it fear? I couldn't be sure. But at that moment, I reasoned it must have been love in some form. How else could anyone endure that, live alongside it, and still stay?

So I expressed my sympathies, careful not to let my own bitterness slip into the words. I tried to keep it neutral, almost distant. After all, this wasn't about the past just yet. We had to find a way to talk before we could even begin to go there.

I suggested we take things slowly, that we start with small steps. It had been too long, and there was too much between us to pretend like we could just fall back into some version of mother and daughter. There were so many things that needed to be worked through, so many conversations that had never been had, and so much pain that hadn't healed. I wasn't ready to dive back into a relationship as if nothing had happened. That wasn't possible; it wasn't even a choice to be had.

I had my own boundaries now, my own sense of self-worth that I'd built over the years apart. Those wounds, the ones I carried from childhood, the ones left by both of them, still felt raw. There were things I needed to say, things I needed to hear, before I could even think about a relationship again. And I needed her to understand that.

I posted my small letter, sealing it with a strange mix of hope and hesitation, and then I waited. I didn't know exactly what I was expecting: a response, a gesture, some kind of acknowledgement. No sooner had I posted the letter than thoughts started to race around my head in circles, each one feeding into the next until it was a full-blown storm in my head. How come she was living somewhere else? Where and what was this new place like?

The curiosity became almost unbearable. I found myself thinking about her new place more and more, wondering what kind of home it was and whether it was anything like the bungalow they'd lived in for so many years. And then something struck me. I hadn't seen their bungalow listed on Rightmove, not once. I'd gotten into the habit of checking the site from time to time, scanning through the listings, not obsessively, but enough to feel like I had a grip on what was going on in their lives, even from a distance. It was my way of keeping an eye on them without actually reaching out. It was a habit I'd picked up after our estrangement, almost like a quiet way of staying connected without the confrontation.

I'd seen my sister's bungalow up for sale a year earlier, and it was just around the corner from my parents, so I noticed it immediately. But their bungalow? Nothing. It hadn't been listed, not once, and that bothered me more than I wanted to admit. My mind, already racing, began piecing things together. Could it be that they had sold it privately? Or maybe they hadn't moved at all, and something else was going on?

It didn't add up. The more I thought about it, the more unsettled I became. My thoughts spiralled into all the possible explanations, some reasonable, others less so.

Maybe they had moved into a care home. Maybe there had been some sort of legal issue with the property. Or, what if something had happened to both of them, and I hadn't been told? It wasn't like my sister would go out of her way to inform me of anything.

My overactive mind wouldn't let it rest. I kept circling back to the same questions, each one more frustrating than the last.

Why hadn't the bungalow been listed?

Jim, always far more tech-savvy than I could ever hope to be, decided to take it upon himself to dig deeper. He could see the restless energy in me, the way I couldn't leave it alone, how I was constantly cycling through theories in my head. He didn't ask me if he should look; he knew instinctively that I needed answers.

He opened his laptop and began searching, his fingers moving quickly across the keys as he navigated various sites and online tools. I watched him from across the room, a mix of anticipation and curiosity stirring within me. I longed for any kind of direction, eager to see what he might uncover.

It didn't take long. I remember the look on his face when he found it, that sudden stillness that fell over him. He glanced at me, and in that split second, I knew something was wrong.

"The bungalow... it burnt down," he said, his voice quiet, almost as if he didn't quite believe the words himself.

I felt my breath catch in my throat. "What do you mean, burnt down?"

He clicked a few more times, then turned the screen towards me. "It's gone. There was a fire. June 2023."

I stared at the screen; a photograph said it all. There stood the burnt-out shell of my parents' home. All that remained standing was a lone side gate made out of wrought iron; it just appeared to stand in thin air, attached to nothing. I was reading the words but not really comprehending them at first. It didn't feel real. My parents' home, the place that I had spent years both running from and yet, in some strange way, always longing to return to, was just… gone. Reduced to ashes in a fire I didn't even know about. The place that held so many complicated memories was no longer standing. I couldn't wrap my head around it.

I had always thought that if I ever went back, I'd be stepping into something familiar, something I knew. But now, there was nothing to return to. The walls that had seen so much and heard so much were gone. A part of me felt an odd sense of loss, but not in the way I expected. It wasn't just the bungalow itself. It was everything it represented. All those unresolved feelings, the part of me that had always imagined walking through that door one last time and facing it all, now felt adrift. There was no door to walk through anymore.

I couldn't speak for a moment, just staring at the screen as if the picture and words might change, as if it might be some mistake. But there it was, clear as day. Jim and I sat there in silence, both of us processing it in our own way.

It felt like a metaphor for everything. The fire, the loss, the way my relationship with Mother and Elaine crumbled over the years; all of it tied together in this one devastating image of the bungalow reduced to nothing. The place that had once held so many memories, tension, pain, was now ash and rubble. There was no going back to confront the past or make sense of it. It was all gone.

As I sat there, staring at the news of the fire, something shifted in me. I had spent so long wrapped up in the anger, the bitterness of everything that had happened, but in that moment, sympathy began to swell unexpectedly in my chest. My mother had been through more than I had realised. Losing Father, the fire, it was more than anyone should have to endure, especially at her age. For the first time in a long while, I could see her as a person who had suffered too, rather than just the distant, emotionally cold figure I had come to associate with my childhood.

Maybe now wasn't the time for slow and careful. Maybe this was a sign that we needed to act, that time was slipping away, and if we waited too long, we'd miss whatever chance we had to salvage something. I didn't know if our relationship could ever be fully repaired, but the thought of leaving it untouched, festering, didn't feel right.

We sent another note, this time more direct, with Jim's phone number included. It felt strange to be offering something so personal after so many years of silence, but it also felt necessary.

Then it happened. Jim walked into the room; as far as I knew he had just left to go to the gym. It turned out that my mother had called him whilst he was driving and he thought it best to return home and let me know. He rang her number and then put her on speakerphone. The moment I heard my mother's voice, coming through the speaker, it stopped me in my tracks. I froze, my body suddenly tense, my heart racing. I've never been one for talking on the phone, especially not in situations as loaded as this one. The idea of hearing her after all these years threw me into a tailspin of anxiety. My mind, as usual, started whirring at a million miles per hour. What would she say? What was I supposed to say? Would it be awkward, strained, or, worse, indifferent? I remained silent.

I had imagined this moment so many times before, running through different versions of it in my head. Maybe she'd sound distant and cold, or maybe she wouldn't want to talk at all. Or maybe, just maybe, she'd express some kind of regret, something that would hint at the possibility of repair. But now that it was actually happening, I was completely unprepared.

With her on loudspeaker, the sound of her voice filled the room. It wasn't what I had expected. She sounded… excited? Giddy, even? "I won't sleep tonight with excitement," she said, and it caught me so off guard that I didn't know how to react. The warmth in her voice was completely at odds with the coldness of the note she had sent. I hadn't heard her sound like this in so long.

As I was drawn in, I felt tears well up in my eyes before I could stop them. Was this real? After all these years of craving her love and seeking her approval in ways I couldn't even explain, was this finally my moment? Could it be that, after everything, she actually wanted me back in her life? That she missed me? My mind raced through a thousand possibilities, but I couldn't quite shake the doubt, the fear, that this was temporary, fleeting.

I didn't know what to say. The idea that she was this happy to hear from me after so much time, after everything that had passed between us, was overwhelming. A part of me wanted to believe it; to hold on to that moment and the hope that maybe, just maybe, things could be different now.

CHAPTER NINETEEN

Facing Her Again

We arranged to visit her the next day. From the moment we ended the call, my stomach churned like a storm was brewing inside me. That night, I lay in bed, staring at the ceiling, my heart pounding in an uneven rhythm, almost as if it was out of sync with the rest of my body. I tossed and turned, trying to prepare myself for what was coming, but no matter how many times I ran through different scenarios in my mind, nothing settled the gnawing anxiety. Every possibility left me with more questions. What would she say? Would there be tension, awkwardness, or, worse, cold indifference? The uncertainty weighed on me like a lead blanket, and by the time the sun rose, I felt as if I hadn't slept at all.

The next morning, we set off, and as we walked through the narrow, winding lanes of Chipping Ongar village, the tension only grew. The pathway beneath my feet felt uneven, each stone crooked and worn by time, as if reflecting the precariousness of the situation. My heart thudded in my chest with every step. I scanned the streets, looking for the address, but nothing felt familiar.

Then we found it. Nestled between two small shops, half-hidden in an alleyway, stood the place. I took it in; this was where my mother lived now. It wasn't at all what I'd imagined. The alley was narrow and shadowed, giving the place an almost forgotten feel, like something you'd walk past without noticing.

A small parking area sat off to the side, leading to a ramp that sloped gently up toward a large, boxy building. It was stark and unremarkable, with heavy, dark-framed glass doors that looked more suited to an office block than a home. The walls were a dull, greyish beige, the kind of colour that made the building seem to blend into the background as if it were trying not to draw attention to itself. There were no personal touches, no flowerpots, no welcome mat and nothing to suggest warmth or familiarity.

As we approached, I felt an odd sense of disconnection. This place, this impersonal structure, was her home. It felt more like outside a waiting room or a clinic, cold, sterile, lacking the cosy details I'd associated with where my mother might live. It was nothing like the small, comfortable bungalow I had pictured in my mind, the kind of place where an elderly woman might settle, surrounded by memories and familiar things. Instead, this definitely felt temporary, like a space she was passing through rather than somewhere she could truly belong.

As we neared the entrance, the glass doors loomed large in front of us, reflecting our distorted figures as we stepped closer. This was it, the moment I had been both dreading and anticipating for years. There was no going back now.

We approached the security system, the metallic panel cold under my fingertips as I pressed her flat number. The moment seemed to stretch out as we stood there waiting for the buzz. My heart pounded louder, and the quiet of the alleyway seemed to amplify every small sound: footsteps in the distance, and the faint whoosh of the wind between the buildings. Then, the door buzzed, breaking the silence. We pushed the large glass door open.

The corridor stretched out in front of us, wide but dimly lit, with walls painted in a sterile off-white. It smelled faintly of cleaning products and something else, a kind of mustiness that comes with old buildings. My footsteps echoed against the hard floor, and as I looked down the hallway, I saw her.

There she stood, at the far end, a tiny figure silhouetted in the faint light spilling through a window behind her. My breath caught in my throat. She was smaller than I remembered, almost shockingly so. Her frame was bent with age, shoulders hunched forward, her arms hanging loosely at her sides. She seemed almost translucent, her skin pale and fragile like delicate parchment stretched too thin over bones. Every step she took was carefully measured, as if the weight of the years bore down heavily on her.

I froze for a moment, taking in the sight of her. This was the woman I had been so desperate to see, the one I had imagined over and over in my mind. But the reality of her, the frailty, the way time had worn her down, hit me harder than I expected. She looked breakable, as if a strong gust of wind might blow her away.

I walked towards her and a lump grew in my throat. The closer I got, the more fragile she seemed, as though time had hollowed her out. The air in the corridor felt thick, almost suffocating, as if the tension from all those lost years had gathered in this small, enclosed space.

When I reached her, I hesitated for a split second, unsure of how to bridge the gap the 11 years had created. But instinctively, I went in for a hug. The gesture felt both familiar and foreign, an automatic response after so long, yet fraught with the weight of everything unsaid. Her body, small and light, folded into mine, and for a moment, I thought she might crumble under the pressure of my embrace. Her frame was so brittle, I loosened my grip, afraid to hold on too tightly, afraid of breaking her.

As I held her, tears slipped down my cheeks, unexpected but uncontrollable. The years of longing, of anger, of resentment all tangled inside me, flooding to the surface. I had craved this connection for so long, yet now that it was happening, it felt overwhelming and surreal. The warmth of her skin, the frailty of her presence, stirred a mixture of grief and relief, of love and hurt. And as I stood there, holding her, I realised how much I had been carrying, how much I had been waiting for this moment, even if I didn't know what to do with it.

Once we stepped inside her flat, I took a deep breath and forced myself to pull it together. I wasn't that scared little girl anymore, the one who had once tiptoed around her moods, afraid of saying the wrong thing. I had grown stronger over the years, stronger through the distance, through the pain, through everything that had happened. And now I had questions – real questions – and I needed answers.

But I knew better than to rush in. Not yet. I watched her carefully, gauging her as she moved slowly about the room. The flat was small, cluttered with things that seemed hastily unpacked, mismatched, and thrown together. It felt impersonal, a far cry from the home I had pictured. She settled herself into a chair, and I followed her lead, taking a seat across from her, resisting the urge to dive straight into what was burning on my mind.

I wasn't sure how much she could handle. She was so old and frail now, physically worn down by time, her hands trembling slightly as she fussed with a cup on the table. But beneath the physical decline, she was still the same woman. Her body had changed, yes, but her mind? That was as sharp as ever where I was concerned. I could see it in her eyes, the same stubbornness, the same iron will that I remembered all too well. Time hadn't touched that part of her.

I felt it deep in my bones; this was not going to be an easy conversation. The sharpness of her gaze, the way she watched me with that same guarded intensity, told me this was going to be delicate. I had to tread carefully, not just for her sake, but for my own. It wasn't just about what I needed to know. It was about navigating all that lay between us.

The room felt soundless, as though even the walls were bracing for the tidal wave of the past that was about to crash over us. It was a silence so thick it seemed to sip into every corner, holding its breath alongside us. Then, all at once, the stillness shattered and the air filled with the awkward hum of overlapping questions, everyone speaking at once, clinging to the polite pretence of asking, How's everybody been?

Mum's voice cut through the jumble, sharp and direct, as always "You're upset, ain't you?"

I paused, her words hanging between us. "I will be alright." The phrase was more for me than for her.

She tilted her head slightly, her gaze unrelenting. "Was you worried about coming?"

I took a deep breath, steadying myself. "I wouldn't say worried," I replied carefully. "More apprehensive."

"So, how many great-grandchildren have I got then?"

With a gentle tone, I replied, "We're not here to upset you, Mum, but we need to cover some ground before we move forward to things like that. It might take some time."

"I was just asking. I don't need to see them or anything," Mum said, her words lingering in the air.

A charged silence filled the room, the weight of her response not lost on any of us. I exchanged a quick glance with Jim, hoping his calm presence would ground us all, knowing the importance of what was about to unravel between Mum and me.

I took a steadying breath. "Again, we're not here to upset you or dig up things just to hurt anyone. But… some things don't go away unless we face them. We've been carrying these memories, these unanswered questions, for far too long."

"It's not easy," Mum admitted, almost to herself, as if the words weren't meant for me to hear. "All these years… I just thought things would sort themselves out, somehow."

I tried to keep my voice gentle, though a tremor of old emotions slipped in. "We've both been through it, Mum. It's not about placing blame, really, but about understanding what happened. Especially for the sake of moving forward, of finding some sort of peace."

Mum murmured that she wasn't very good with words.

"It's not about the words, Mum," I said softly. "It's about the space we're making here now, what we do with everything left unsaid."

I told Mum that we knew about the fire.

"How did you hear about it?" she asked, knowing full well she hadn't told us herself. We explained, and then I asked her about it.

Her first words were, "I got pulled out of the window."

Mother and Father had just had a row. The last words she said to him before he stormed off to the garage were, "Either you leave, or I'm going to." Mum then retreated to one of the bedrooms at the front of the bungalow. She continued, "Funnily enough, April, I was reading your old letters, and all was quiet as hell. Then I heard this big bang! I got off the bed and went to the window to see if I could see anything, and there was black smoke billowing past the glass."

I couldn't believe what I was hearing. I just sat there, listening. Mother continued, "The next thing I knew, the neighbours were outside shouting at me to open the window. So I did, even though at that point I still didn't know what was going on. The neighbours got me out, and as I looked around, I could see the whole cul-de-sac filled with cars and people who'd come to watch. There were so many, they couldn't get an ambulance or fire engine down there."

Mum paused for a minute, almost to collect her memories, and then continued in earnest. "I asked where Frank was; I didn't want to leave him, and then all of a sudden, there he was, curled up on the driveway in the front garden. His head was burnt, and so were his arm and hand. It was like everything we had had come crashing down."

She shifted slightly, her tone taking a different direction. "He was near-blind by then, you know. Nearly all the way gone. He was obviously trying to clean out some old paint pot in the garage, I reckon. Must've thought lighting it would help him see if it was empty. Stupid thing to do, really."

A heaviness settled in my chest, questions swirling in my mind from the past few days, wondering why no one had told us. I tried to steady my voice. "Mum, we didn't know. No one told us what had happened."

It wasn't hard to imagine, the chaos, the fear, her watching the life she'd known go up in flames. A flood of vivid images filled my mind.

She continued, "Elaine was in Billericay the evening it happened. She got a call from her daughter's mother-in-law, who lives a street away. 'I can see smoke coming from the direction of where you live,' she told Elaine. Elaine's first concern was for her two dogs that were home alone. She didn't get back until late, only to find out it wasn't her bungalow that had burnt down, but mine."

Mum digressed, her tone shifting. "We'd been told to get our money out of the bank, you know, because as you get older, they take 40% inheritance tax."

She looked directly at Jim, knowing full well I wouldn't understand such matters. "You know about this?" she asked him. Jim nodded.

"Elaine had been advised to get all the money out, and I'd stuffed it away in different places in the bungalow. I was trying to stop her, saying, 'I don't want any more money in this bungalow,' but she wouldn't listen.

"Luckily, I'd told her everywhere I'd hidden it," Mum said, "and she managed to go in afterwards, once the firemen had damped it down. She got every penny."

Jim asked, "Did she put it back in the bank?"

Mum chuckled. "I'm not going near a bank anymore."

She went on to explain how the bungalow wasn't insured. "Elaine went and got the money before she even knew whether we were dead or alive. It was only the firemen who gave her any information."

I asked Mum, "Why weren't you insured?"

"We always had house insurance, but when it came up for renewal, we thought, why bother? We'd never had a fire in all these years, and we probably wouldn't be around much longer. So, we decided to save the money," Mum said.

I couldn't help but think that if Elaine had been looking after them properly, she should have made sure they at least had house insurance. But no, everyone was too focused on saving money, it seemed.

The conversation shifted to how Mum had come to live in this new place.

"Elaine found it," Mum said.

"And this is where you've been ever since?" I asked.

"Yeah. I wasn't much help, Elaine sorted it all. Elaine's done her bit, I'll say that. Comes regularly to make sure I'm not dead yet!" A flicker of wry humour crossed her face, a brief return of her usual bluntness.

Jim gave a quiet chuckle, and I felt him shift beside me. "That sounds like Elaine," he said lightly, his tone warm.

Mum's expression turned serious again. "I didn't want to leave, not really. But there wasn't much left to leave behind after the fire."

Saying his name felt heavy, but I went for it. "And Frank?" I asked.

"He lasted a few weeks after we moved here," Mum said. "His health was already poor, and the fire just seemed to take the last bit of fight out of him. After he passed, it was… I don't know. It felt like an end, in more ways than one."

"You've been through a lot, Jo," Jim said gently. "Elaine has been there for you, which is good. But April's here too, and I think we both know it's not fair to keep her at arm's length."

"You're right," Mum replied, her voice softening. "Sometimes, it just feels easier to let the past lie. I've been carrying it all for too long."

I took a steady breath, willing my voice to stay even. "Mum, we can't keep running away from it. Maybe it's time to stop hiding, to finally look at what's there."

Mother gave a small nod, her expression one of quiet resignation. "Maybe you're right, maybe it's time I stopped running. I didn't mean for it to happen this way, you know," she said, her gaze fixed on some distant point in the room.

Then, changing the subject, she added, "There were days that I wondered if I would ever see you again, April. Wondered if you'd come back or if I'd gone and lost you for good." Her voice grew soft, almost apologetic, though she didn't look directly at me.

144

"Mum, I didn't leave because I wanted to," I said, my words catching in my throat. "I left because I needed… I needed to find a way to feel whole for the first time in my life. Everything I'd been through… it was draining me of my sanity. It wasn't fair on my family. When I wasn't heard by you, it was my family who had to bear the brunt of it all and pick up the pieces."

"I know," she whispered, her voice barely audible. "I didn't understand it then. But I think I do now. Things were difficult, and you did what you thought was best."

We sat in silence, letting the weight of those words settle between us.

I was in shock. These were the closest words I'd ever had to an acknowledgement in my entire life. Hope stirred within me, fragile and tentative, but I knew better than to let it take hold too quickly. Mum had a way of swiping it away in an instant.

Was something easing between us? A fragile truce forming in the space where our words had just lingered? Maybe, just maybe, this was how it would be different now.

I could see her mind shifting, stirring those memories she'd buried for so long.

"It wasn't easy," she said finally, her voice trembling slightly. "Your father… he had his ways. And sometimes I just… I didn't know what else to do. I thought, if I kept things quiet, if I just stayed out of his way… maybe it would be enough."

There were questions bubbling up now, ones I couldn't hold back any longer. "What did you tell people, Mum? About why I wasn't around?"

145

She replied in her usual blunt tone, "I just told them, 'I do not want to talk about it.'"

"And how do you see things now, from my perspective?" I pressed gently.

She hesitated, then said, "I think Frank's death brought me to my senses. I haven't cried a tear over him, you know. Not one. Whenever he wanted to talk about the subject, I'd shut him up, I'd get him off it. I couldn't handle it and didn't want to handle anything. That's why it all happened."

She admitted, finally, to blocking me out. "I just hated the subject."

I took a steadying breath, then brought up something that had weighed on me for years. "You've always favoured Elaine, Mum. You've given her so much more, especially financially."

Her reply came swiftly. "Elaine was always more *ambitious* than you, and you never asked. We never turned Elaine down. If you had asked, I would have given to you too."

That one, spoken so matter-of-factly, quietly infuriated me. I knew all too well it wasn't true. But, determined to keep the tone calm, especially since we seemed to be making progress, I simply declared, "We'll have to agree to disagree on that one."

I took a breath and explained, as plainly as I could, the meaning of fairness. "It's about being equal, Mum. We don't give to Emma without also giving to Louise."

Mum's response was blunt, as always. "I was too busy just getting by to be thinking about being fair," she said.

Mum continued, "It's funny, isn't it? You think you'll be a certain kind of mother, and then life gets in the way. There were things I thought I'd get around to, things I'd fix. But the years… they just slip by, don't they?"

Her words struck a chord, pulling at the constant memories I'd spent years trying to untangle. I thought of the letter I'd written to her, the one she'd recently mentioned finding. It had been a desperate attempt, a final push to be seen by her, to make her understand.

And now, here we were. For the first time, it felt like she was meeting me halfway, acknowledging the distance that had shaped our relationship all those years.

Her words stirred fragments of childhood memories, vivid and unrelenting. Moments when I had tried to connect with her, hoping for warmth, for something real to hold on to. But those attempts had often left me feeling emptier, like I'd reached out and found nothing but air.

When Mum said again, "We cannot change the past," I replied gently, "No, we can't, Mum. But we can change how we view it."

I told Mum, "You had your mum, your dad, Bill, Bet, Tom, June or Pat to turn to. I was a child and had absolutely no one."

She hesitated, then admitted, "You were forced to live in a situation without me caring about it… or anything."

Her words, raw and unguarded, struck something deep in me. "All I ever wanted, Mum, was for you to understand me," I said, my voice trembling with longing.

We'd been on "the subject" long enough, and I wanted to shift away from it, ease the tension and leave Mum on a good note. Steering the conversation towards more pleasant updates from the last 11 years, I began, "Jim's retired now."

"When did you retire?" she asked, sounding genuinely curious.

"Two years ago," Jim replied.

"When Jim retired, we decided to renovate the house," I added, pulling out my phone to show her pictures of how it looked now.

Mum studied the images for a moment. "So, you've taken an old house and modernised it," she said.

Somehow, the conversation drifted to Elaine, and I felt compelled to tell Mum that I had my grievances with her. "I don't expect you to get in the middle of it," I said, keeping my tone steady.

Before we wrapped up and arranged a time to visit her the following week, I let her know she had four great-grandchildren. Her eyes widened with surprise, clearly blown away by the news.

Then Mum mentioned that Sally, Elaine's daughter, was having a baby. "We already knew," Jim said casually.

Mum's expression shifted. "How do you know that?" she asked, her tone sharpening.

"Jim looked on the internet a couple of days ago," I explained.

Her reply came quickly, harsh and defensive. "So you've been nosing into everything about me?"

Jim gently showed her the article about the fire online, as if to soften her reaction. "We don't know everything," he reassured her.

The last thing I did before we left was show her a picture of our four grandchildren. Her face lit up with delight, and for a moment, the room felt lighter too.

"Blimey, you've got big money, big family, big house, ain't ya?" Mum said, her tone a mix of curiosity and directness. "Can't get any higher, what are you going to look forward to now?"

We reassured her quickly. "Plenty to keep us busy," Jim said with a smile. "The grandchildren alone are enough to keep us on our toes."

The conversation shifted again as Mum focused on Jim, and admitted, somewhat reluctantly, that she'd found something out on the internet about his business through Elaine. "Apparently, the firm went bust?" she said, her tone defensive. I didn't say it, but thought , *So it's okay for her to be nosey, but not us!*

Jim chuckled and set the record straight. "That's not the case at all," he said, his voice calm as he explained.

I reminded Mother of the six letters we exchanged after the "car incident". She immediately shot back, "I said I'd meet you in Brentwood," but she was getting muddled. Her thoughts were drifting back to 2010, the start of her pushing me away. Back then, she didn't want to turf Father out of his own home, so she suggested meeting in Brentwood, but I said I'd come pick her up and bring her over to ours for the day. Which I did, right up until the day I screamed at her to 'get out of the car'.

Much to my surprise, Mother gave me a glimmer of hope. "If you can produce those letters," she said, "I'll be truly sorry for everything."

I was stunned, and, for the first time, excited by what Mother had to say. This was an easy task for me. I know exactly where they are. "I'll bring them with me next time." I was happy to leave the subject on that note.

After a long pause, we stood up to leave. Mum looked over at Jim and me, and her tone softened. "Maybe we can start anew," she said, almost hesitantly. "Build some new memories."

"Maybe," I replied.

Jim added gently, "Perhaps we should let you rest now, it's been a lot for you to take in today."

She looked up at him appreciatively. "Thank you, Jim. And thank you, April, for coming."

If nothing else, that day I glimpsed another side of Mum. The side I should have encountered 57 years ago, when I first tried to tell her what Father was doing to me. Maybe it was because I had given her the space to be a victim that day, after everything she'd recently been through, that she was finally able to acknowledge that I too had been a victim for all these years. Or maybe she had truly missed me and knew she had to give a little to keep me there.

As much as I wanted to believe this was a good start, I couldn't let myself fall hook, line, and sinker into thinking everything would suddenly be okay. Mum had let me down too many times before.

Still, I concluded that the day had gone as well as it possibly could. For now, I could hold on to hope.

CHAPTER TWENTY

It's All Just a Joke to Her

"Five onions, not big ones, little ones, £2.00." She chuckled, shaking her head. "I didn't realise until I went to pay, bleating hell, everyone jumping on the bandwagon!"

We were firmly on Mother's favourite subject: a bargain, with an added gripe for good measure. From there, the conversation stayed on everyday topics for the next forty minutes, the kind of light chatter that keeps the peace, with no sharp edges or unexpected turns. It was almost a relief to let the conversation settle into safer, simpler territory. Neutral ground that felt safe. Then, I decided it was time to steer the conversation toward what had been on my mind.

"Mum, did you retain any of what we spoke about last week?" I asked carefully.

She laughed, the sound a mix of self-deprecation and dismissal. "Oh, I have difficulty remembering things. Tell you the truth, I got it shoved down me so quick I can't remember it." Jim chuckled softly, breaking the tension, but I stayed focused.

This week, Mother is determined to make light of things. I explain to her, "The abuse at Father's hands didn't stop until I got married."

Mother says, "Sounds like he did you a favour."

Her attempt at humour lands with a thud, and she quickly reprimands herself. "I'm just trying to make light of it because we can't keep going on like this," she says.

I press on, telling her how everything I had endured made it nearly impossible for me to trust anyone along the way.

"Nor do I," Mother replies, laughing. "Not when they put their prices up." She was referring to her onions, again.

I was floored that Mum could so effortlessly brush off my trauma and twist it into a joke about her shopping. Stunned, I decided to shift gears, desperate for even a brief reprieve.

Mum carried on, her tone light but resolute. "I know what the trouble is, but what can we do about it? Nothing."

I could feel the weight of the long slog that lay ahead. This wasn't going to be easy, but there was no avoiding it. "One thing I know you haven't forgotten, Mum, because you've brought it up so much," I said, steadying myself, "is how I shouted at you, telling you to get out of the car."

"Yeah," she replied, her voice softening. "I remember saying that last week."

"Do you remember me explaining why I acted like that?" I pressed gently.

"It was something that started over the girls' weddings, I know that," she said, almost as if testing the waters of her own memory.

"About the weddings, you understand why you weren't invited, don't you?" I asked her.

She looked at me blankly. "No," she said, without a hint of hesitation.

I tried to explain. "Some people have strong views on certain subjects, and they might have said something to you. I didn't want to risk that happening."

Her response was instant, dismissive. "I would've told them it's none of their bloody business." She refused to acknowledge that I was protecting *her*, and that I didn't want to take any chances with that kind of behaviour at our daughters' weddings. But she wouldn't see it that way, no matter how much I tried to explain.

I took a breath and tried again. "It wasn't just about the wedding, Mum. It came from years and years of frustration. Not just from one situation, but from not being heard for so long. That's what built up to that moment."

She hesitated, her tone shifting. "I didn't realise that, April."

"Are you grasping what I'm saying now?" I asked, leaning forward, my voice tinged with hope.

"It's had a deep effect on you, but once it's done, nobody, me, Jim, or you, can undo it. It has to be overlooked," Mother said.

"Mum," I began, "it can be overlooked to a certain extent, but only once I feel I have been understood."

Silence.

Exhausted, I changed the subject. "Can I ask what you said to Elaine about our visit last week, Mum?"

"I said I was disappointed," she replied. "You wanted the truth, don't you? I was disappointed because I was looking forward to it so much, and it turned into... well, an interrogation."

A wave of emotions crashed over me, starting with a sharp pang of sadness. My stomach tightened. Was I adding to her grief after everything she had been through? Had our visit been another burden, another weight on her already heavy shoulders? Disappointment followed close behind, a heavy ache settling in my chest as I realised she truly believed we could simply move on. The memory of last week's visit, once a beacon of hope, now felt tainted with a sense of falseness, a performance rather than genuine reconciliation. And then, the familiar sting of injustice – the feeling that, once again, *I* was the one to blame.

We fell into a new conversation, the way we often did, steering clear of the past. Instead, we talked about my brother. She always liked to talk about him. He was the one person in the family I never hated. How could I? He was caught up in his own world, his own battles, and none of it was his fault.

Mum didn't see it that way, though. To her, my brother's quirks, his schizophrenia, and his OCD were something she could easily wrap her head around. There was comfort in talking about it. It made more sense to her than what had happened to me.

"He was always meticulous," she said, a hint of pride in her voice.

I could see it too, the way he used to fuss over every crumb. If Elaine or I dared eat a biscuit, he'd watch with hawk-like precision, waiting for even the tiniest fragment to fall. And when it did, he'd swoop in, frantic to clean every last one. As if the world would fall apart if he didn't.

That's how he was with everything: obsessive, controlled, his own mind spinning out of his control.

I nodded, picturing him in those moments, half-frustrated, half-amused by how over-the-top he could get. But the stories didn't stop at crumbs. My brother's life had been full of unexpected moments.

There was that one night. Out of nowhere, he ended up in Scotland. No money to his name. Mum still couldn't quite understand how he had managed it. He'd told staff at every station that he'd pay them back next time he passed through. Somehow, that charm got him all the way to the far north of the country. It was absurd, yet it made perfect sense. That was my brother. Always a story to tell.

But even with all his quirks, I never held any of it against him. He was in the middle of his own chaos. And while it spun around him, trapping him in its orbit, it wasn't his fault.

And it wasn't mine either.

Our parents, though, they never saw it that way. To them, it was as if nothing else mattered. In the earlier years they were always focused on him, wrapped up in the whirlwind of his needs, his care. Elaine and I, were the background noise, there, but not really seen, our needs always secondary to the turmoil unfolding around us.

It wasn't that I wanted them to love him less or to stop worrying about him. But growing up in a family where all the attention was diverted elsewhere, where you were expected to just cope because *he* needed more, it left its mark. I learned early on how to be invisible, how to stay quiet, because that's what was expected of me.

As Mum spoke, her voice softening at the mention of his name, I couldn't help but wonder how much of that attention was given out of love, and how much was given out of guilt. It was as though focusing on my brother allowed them to ignore everything else. To ignore me. To ignore what happened.

They were too wrapped up in his struggles to see mine.

It's funny how much power silence holds, even years after the fact. We sat there in Mum's lounge, her talking on and on about my brother, and I kept quiet, as I always had. It was easier that way. Easier than confronting the truth. Easier than asking the questions I never dared to.

But the silence persevered. And in moments like this, it was almost unbearable. Because as much as I wanted to join in, to talk about my brother like he was the only story that mattered, I knew deep down that there were so many other stories, mine included, that had been brushed aside, forgotten, ignored.

Mum's focus was always elsewhere, on the things she could understand, on the things that had easier explanations. My brother's illness, his quirks, his odd behaviours – they were tangible, they were visible. My pain? My story? That was something she couldn't, or *wouldn't,* see.

And even now, as we talked, as she shared stories about him with a fondness I hadn't seen in years, I had to remind myself of what she chose to ignore. What she *allowed* to happen.

Because that was the story she wouldn't tell.

CHAPTER TWENTY-ONE

Meeting Back Up With Elaine

This was my third visit to Mother's flat in as many weeks, but today felt different. Elaine was going to be there, my sister, whom I hadn't seen in thirteen years. My heart raced as we pulled up, but I wasn't afraid. This time, I was ready. Thirteen years apart had made me stronger, clearer, and determined. Taking a deep breath, I stepped inside, resolved to face whatever awaited me.

It started as these things often do: with questions. Questions that had lingered for years in a place where relationships once were.

"Why weren't you in contact?" I asked Elaine, the words tumbling out with a mix of curiosity and resignation.

Elaine didn't hesitate. "Don't know, why weren't you in contact?"

"Are you going to turn this around?" I asked.

"No, no," she said, cutting me off with the sharpness only my sister can manage. "I'm not going to turn this around. We've got questions; this isn't just some general chat."

"Questions?" I repeated, more for myself than her. "It's not all about questions, Elaine." But my words didn't matter.

"For years," she pressed on, "I sent Christmas cards. I don't even know what I did to deserve being cut off, but I kept sending them. And I never got anything back." Her voice cracked slightly, betraying her practiced indignation. "Not a word."

I let out a slow breath. "Christmas cards?" The memory didn't sit right with me.

"Yes," she insisted. "I remember I sent them for a couple of years. Then I gave up. I thought, 'What's the point?'"

"We all remember things differently," I offered, trying to find some neutral ground.

"Fine," she snapped, "but why did you cut Sally out? What did she ever do? Tell me."

Her questions weren't questions; they were accusations, about why I hadn't been in touch with her daughter.

"Well, what did Emma and Louise do?" I retorted.

"I thought I wrote to them, sent them cards on those first birthdays, or whatever it was," Elaine said.

"No, I think you'll find you'd given up on them before that. You stopped giving the birthday and Christmas presents when Emma was 17 and Louise was 14. There were no more Christmas presents or anything for them from you, and you only have the two nieces," I replied.

"They had got older at that point," Elaine said, as if that excused her.

"So you stop sending birthday cards just because they get older?" I asked.

"Regardless, I remember sending Christmas cards, and when I heard nothing for a couple of years, I gave up," Elaine said.

I replied, "Well, I can honestly say there's no recollection of that."

If nothing else, we agreed that we would all have different memories.

Jim reminded Elaine that he'd initially contacted her using her work email address, since we didn't have any other contact details for her. After Elaine responded to that email, Jim called her at work, and they spoke for some time. During their conversation, Jim asked Elaine how she, their mother, and Terrance were doing. Elaine later confirmed that this conversation had taken place. This email exchange and phone call occurred in 2014. At the end of the call, Elaine agreed she would let Mother know we'd been in touch, and she says she did pass the message on.

However, just like my last letter to my mother, asking her to keep in touch, there was no response. Nothing.

Jim pointed out to Elaine that, by her own admission, she had not sent any Christmas cards since 2012.

Elaine deflected "But Sally, why was she cut out?" as though her daughter was an exception to everything.

I cut in, "So would you like me to be part of Sally's life and tell her the truth of what happened?"

An eerie silence filled the room.

"What are you talking about? Dad?" Elaine asked hesitantly.

"Yeah," I said flatly.

In an unearthly tone, Elaine replied, "If you'd like to." She then quickly deflected again. "But why did you suddenly cut her out?"

"Because I cut myself off from everybody, in order to protect everybody else," I said.

Elaine narrowed her eyes. "Protect everybody else from what?"

"From the lies," I said, the words stinging even as they left my mouth. "Why did you tell lies about me?"

She looked confused. "Lies? What lies, April?"

I didn't want to say it. But it hung there between us, demanding acknowledgement. "Father's funeral," I finally said. "Why wasn't I there? You told everyone it was because of a family dispute. Do you know how that made me look? Everyone else was there: Jackie, your friend from school, Ryan – everyone. And I wasn't. It made me look like the problem," I said. "And why should I be seen in a bad light for not knowing about the fire?" I asked.

"That doesn't put you in a bad light," Elaine said, her voice softening. "Whenever people asked where you were, I simply told them it was a family dispute. I didn't make you look in a bad light."

"But you did," I said, feeling my composure slipping. "You could have told them the truth. You could have told them that Frank sexually abused me. Instead, Elaine, you told Penny without asking me!"

"I share a house with Penny," Elaine said defensively. "Of course I told her. What was I supposed to do?"

"And yet, when I tell anyone, when I tell my daughters, it's somehow wrong," I shot back. "I'm the one who's condemned for it."

Elaine shifted uncomfortably. "I didn't want to spread the truth around, April. I was trying to protect Mum."

I could not help but think, Elaine was more interested in protecting the money than protecting Mother.

"And I've never protected Mum?" I shot back.

"I guess you have… April, you seem very aggravated."

If I wasn't before, I was now. A burning rage ignited inside me as she continued to throw in her two pennies' worth, trying to derail what I was attempting to say. I took a deep breath to calm myself.

"I am calm, and I intend to stay calm. I'm not about to give you the satisfaction of me losing it," I said.

I believe what was happening in this moment to be called 'gaslighting'.

Elaine sighed deeply. "I don't know what you want from me. You've clearly got a lot of grievances with me. Is that why you cut me out?"

I nodded. "Yes, Elaine. That's part of it." Something I had reminded Elaine many times over the years: "You took the moral high ground, didn't you? You said you could do whatever you wanted with your life, and no one could criticise, condemn or frown upon you after what Frank did to me. And you did exactly that."

"I don't know," Elaine whispered. "Maybe I said that. I don't remember, sounds like something I would say."

"You took them for everything you could, Elaine," I said, my voice trembling. "You took a trip to Canada, then Wales, racked up online debts, had Father set up a shop for you, did a lot of work on your first flat, sorted out a house for you, from which they lost loads of money, and they bought a house and rented it out cheaply to you. That is just the half of it. And what did I get? Nothing."

Mum chimed in, "You should have done the same, April." She was talking utter rubbish. She'd conveniently

161

forgotten how she'd once turned up at our door, handed me £20, and said they weren't going to "buy me", after everything he'd done. And she'd clearly erased from memory the one time we'd asked for help, when she'd flat-out refused us. Now here she was, casually claiming I could've simply asked for help. Yeah, right!

Elaine shook her head. "But I don't see what this has to do with anything. I used to get Dad to do lots of work for me." She said it as if he'd simply been fulfilling his fatherly duties, conveniently overlooking the fact that this "work" had been ongoing, almost non-stop, for forty years.

Elaine continued. "Okay, so I benefited from Mum and Dad. I took advantage of what Dad could do because I couldn't afford it myself, and he lived just around the corner most of those times. He had the skills and knowledge, and it saved me money."

We pointed out to her that we'd received no help at all.

"No," I said firmly, "but you can at least admit it. Admit that you used him. You took everything, while I got nothing."

For a moment, there was silence. Then Elaine whispered, "I did what I had to do."

Her voice became barely audible as she added, "I suppose, if I were in your shoes, I'd feel exactly the same way."

Her words lingered in the air. And for the first time in a long time, I felt like we were standing on the same ground, however uneven it might be. We started talking about when Elaine told the school about Father abusing me.

"I remember going to the school," she said finally. "I used it as my outlet, a chance to tell someone, anyone. That's how it came out. That's how Mum found out."

"So it wasn't for yourself?" I asked, my voice quieter now.

"No," she said firmly. "It was about what was happening at home with my sister. I hoped that by telling someone, they'd do something. But they didn't." She shook her head as though trying to erase the memory. "It was different back then. Things aren't like that now. If it happened today, there'd be people, services, funding. But back then, nothing."

Her words landed like stones in my chest, and I couldn't help myself. "It's ironic, isn't it?" I said, my voice sharper than I intended. "You, of all people, with the job you do now you fully understand how a child feels, how they react to being abused by a parent. You know how silence destroys a child. And yet, you've shown no understanding or compassion for me as your sister, as a victim of that same abuse."

"Sadly," Elaine said with a shrug, "I didn't see it that way. We weren't talking, so there was nothing to fix."

"Do you remember when I went to the psychiatrist? When the doctor recommended I go, and I told you and Mum?"

Elaine's face was blank.

"They wanted the whole family there: him, Mother and you," I reminded her. "But you came to my door and told me that no one would be attending. Do you remember that, Elaine?"

Her silence was deafening.

"I know what psychiatrists do," I continued. "They sit, they listen, and they try to help. And yet, when I needed you, you were nowhere to be found."

Elaine said, "As far as I was concerned, I didn't have a sister; you just disappeared. I didn't know what I had done, so I just thought, 'sod you'; it doesn't matter what my job is."

I felt the sting of her words but refused to let them derail me. "Everything goes back to him," I said. "Back to Father. You know that, don't you?"

"Of course I do," she said quickly. "But I can't change what he did." She sounded just like Mother.

"No one can," I said. "But you could have supported me. You could have helped me get through it."

Elaine deflected and said, "You know Mother can be blunt."

"That doesn't make it okay," I said. "You have to understand, Elaine, that when Mum talks about what she went through, how she kept the family together, it's all about her. There's nothing in there for me. Nothing about what I went through."

Jim, silent until now, finally spoke. His voice was calm, but firm. "But what about April?" he asked, looking straight at Elaine. "You all knew that she wasn't an independent type of person. *Someone who would not survive alone.* For eleven years, no one got in touch with her. She could've been dead. I could've left her. She could have been a drug addict, and no one would have known because no one bothered to reach out."

Elaine flinched but held her ground. "I didn't know," she said weakly. "I didn't think to get in touch." Elaine went on to say, "Mum made her choices. I know that. I do. And I understand why you feel the way you do.

"I've tried to explain things to her," she said. "But she's stubborn. And blunt. You know that."

Blunt. That was always one way of putting it. I sighed. "You talk about Mum's struggle," I said, "but do you even know what it's been like for me? I've been protecting her, all of you, for my whole life. And yet, I've never had anyone protecting me. I've lived with this for decades, Elaine. And it's exhausting."

"I know," she said, "I get that now. But you have to understand, it wasn't easy for any of us."

Her words stung, not because they were untrue, but because they only skimmed the surface.

"Do you know what Mum said to me recently?" I asked, my voice trembling. "She said, 'Why couldn't it have always been like this?' But then, without missing a beat, she added, 'But it couldn't, could it? Because I chose him over you.' Can you even imagine how that felt, hearing her say those words?"

Elaine didn't answer. She just stared down at her hands, her silence deafening.

"You know, if I hadn't met him…" I began, referring to Jim, but Elaine tried to interrupt. I quickly cut her off. "Do you have any idea where I'd be right now?"

Elaine answered casually, almost dismissively, "You're going to say you wouldn't be alive."

Mother stayed silent.

"But you've got a strong guy who has been there for you and looked after you," Elaine said.

"And that makes it right?" I shot back. "And the letters," I continued, the words spilling out now. "Do you even remember the letters? Mum and I exchanged six letters in total, and she claimed she couldn't recall them."

"I didn't know about that," Elaine murmured. "I never saw them."

"Of course you didn't," I said sarcastically. "When Mum replied to one of my letters, she mentioned you'd just walked in and even added a comment from you. Yet she couldn't bring herself to answer any of my questions. Three times I wrote to her. Three times I asked. And each time, nothing. She ignored them all, Elaine. Do you know what I think?" I leaned back, my arms crossed. "I think she didn't want to leave a trail. She didn't want anything in writing because that would've been evidence."

Elaine looked up, her face pale. "Evidence of what?"

"Evidence of *everything*." I said simply. "Evidence of what I went through. Evidence of Father sexually abusing me. Of what Mum allowed to happen, and what *you* took advantage of."

Elaine didn't deny it. Instead, she nodded slowly. "You're probably right," she admitted. "But I don't think she saw it that she was allowing it. Mum just stayed silent."

Little did I know, Elaine was holding her own silence.

I shook my head, feeling anger bubbling beneath my skin. "For eleven years," I said, "I've been waiting – waiting for someone to reach out, to acknowledge what happened to me. But nobody ever did. All these years, I've searched

166

everywhere for comfort: quotes, sayings, anything to make sense of this mess. Do you know what I read the other day? 'Having your trauma constantly invalidated and dismissed creates wounds that need just as much healing as the trauma itself.' That's been my life, Elaine. That's exactly what I've had to live with."

Elaine dropped her gaze, her shoulders slumping under the weight of my words. "I get it," she said softly. "I do. I really do."

"Do you?" I asked, my voice barely above a whisper.

"In what way do those quotes even comfort you?" she asked gently.

"Because they validate how I feel. Because I've always felt like the outsider. There's a quote I found that sums it up perfectly: 'The survivor of abuse wears the heart of an orphan.' Tell me that's not true. I've had no aunts, no uncles, no cousins; I've had nobody."

Elaine tried to interrupt, but I quickly cut her off. Anger burned beneath my skin, a rage I was struggling desperately to contain. "You know, I almost bumped into Sally once. She was standing at the top of the escalator at Lakeside, and I just managed to sidestep her. Tell me, what was I supposed to say to her?"

A tense silence filled the room before I continued, fighting to keep my voice steady. "And while we're on the subject of Sally, why did you leave her with Mum and Father when you knew exactly what he'd done to me?"

The silence thickened, becoming almost unbearable. Oblivious as ever, Mother broke the tension with a puzzled, "Why's it suddenly gone so quiet?"

167

Jim opened his mouth to speak, but I stopped him with a sharp gesture, my voice trembling with barely contained fury. "I've asked Elaine a question, and I want an answer."

Silence again. Then Elaine said something that shattered my entire reality.

"It happened to Sally." Her voice broke like glass.

You could have heard a pin drop.

"What do you mean it happened to Sally?" I asked.

"It happened to Sally," Elaine said, her voice cracking.

"What, by Father?" I asked.

"Yeah,", she said.

"You let that happen?" I said, the fury inside me now building.

I felt the air being sucked out of the room. My body went rigid, as if bracing for a blow I couldn't see coming. I stared at her, searching her face for... what? Denial? Deflection? But no, it was there, clear as day – guilt. The weight of it was etched into every line on her face.

"You're saying Frank, our father, sexually abused your daughter too?" I asked, my voice barely a whisper. My heart was pounding so hard I thought I might pass out.

Elaine nodded, and her lips trembled as she spoke again. "Yes," she said, her voice faltering but resolute. "It happened."

I closed my eyes, the confirmation slicing through me like a knife. My body felt too small to contain the surge of emotions – rage, despair, disbelief – that tore through me all at once. "And you let that happen?" I whispered again, my voice shaking. "You knew. You knew what he was capable of, what he did to me. And you still left her with him?"

Elaine turned extremely nasty. "April, I swear, I didn't think that would happen again."

"You didn't think?" The words erupted from me, sharp and furious. I was trying to contain the storm inside me. "You didn't think? After everything I went through, after everything you saw, you didn't think?"

"I wasn't the same person back then," she said, her voice breaking. "I wasn't trained. I didn't understand it the way I do now. I thought it was… over. It had been thirty years, April. Thirty years. It didn't even cross my mind that he would do it again."

"That's not good enough!" I shouted, my voice reverberating through the room. "You are her mother. It was your job to protect her. To keep her safe. And you failed her. You failed her, Elaine!"

Elaine's shoulders sagged under the weight of my words. "I wasn't trying to hurt her," she said, her voice barely above a whisper. "I was trying to escape my own mess. To get away from Ted. To build a better life for us. I didn't think he would do it again. I didn't think…"

"You didn't think." The bitterness in my voice was palpable. "You didn't think about her. Or me. Or anyone, only yourself. You were so busy thinking of yourself that you handed your daughter over to him like a lamb to the slaughter."

"Stop it!" Elaine cried, her hands flying to her ears. "I know, okay? I know. Don't you think I know? I've been living with this guilt for years, April. Sally barely speaks to me now. She spends all her time in counselling, trying to undo the damage I let happen. And it's my fault. I know it's my fault."

Elaine then said, "I remember you coming to the house at Kelvedon Hatch, mentioning him working, and I clearly recall saying to you, 'I'm going to get everything I can out of him!'" I remembered this vividly too, because that comment, made just before the puppy incident, was the final straw for me. I was completely done watching Elaine continually receive his help, and now even her "friend" was benefiting. This highlighted Elaine's willingness to conceal the truth from me and how aggressively she pursued Father to ensure she got the most out of him.

Elaine continued to trip over her own words. She then became extremely aggressive again. "And anyway, I want to know why you left my daughter with him?"

I was stunned; was she really blaming me for what happened to *her* daughter? Had I just heard right? I took a minute to absorb what she had just said. Mystified, I said, "Unbelievable, I am going to wake up in a minute!"

Her voice cracked, and she collapsed into a chair, her body shaking with sobs. For a moment, I just sat there, staring at her. My sister. The person who should have been my ally, my protector. All I could feel was anger, and betrayal. And the searing ache of all the things that had been taken from me, and now from her daughter, Sally.

"I wish I could go back," Elaine finally said, her voice choked with regret. "I wish I could go back and change everything. But I can't. And I'm so sorry, April, for Sally, for you, for all of it."

Her apology lingered between us, fragile and uncertain. I wanted to accept it, to ease some of the burden from her shoulders, but I couldn't. The wounds ran too deep, the scars still too raw.

Elaine began opening up about the moment she'd told Sally about how our father had sexually abused me.

"I think there was always a fear," Elaine began slowly, carefully choosing her words. "A fear of telling Sally about what happened to you. I just didn't know… I didn't know how to do it – how to even bring it up."

Elaine swallowed hard, her face pale. "I told Sally on her 18th birthday. Even though you and I weren't speaking, April, I decided she was old enough to know. I couldn't keep it from her any longer."

The weight of that revelation must have been too much for Sally. As a trauma response, she'd gone straight out, gotten drunk, and ended up being charged with drink driving. Elaine hadn't exactly been open about that part; we'd stumbled across it online some time ago. Now, suddenly, everything added up.

"But Sally had already told you about her own abuse before you told her, hadn't she?" I asked, my voice trembling.

Elaine nodded slowly. "Yes, she had. She told me when she was very young, about eight or nine. I don't know how long it had been going on or all the exact details. But the moment she started talking, I just knew. I didn't question her. I didn't say, 'Are you sure?' or anything like that. The second she began speaking, my heart sank. I thought, he's done it again."

Her words pierced my heart. I clenched my fists tightly, fighting to stay composed. "And what did you do then?" I asked, forcing myself to look her in the eyes.

"I went straight down there," Elaine said, her voice cracking. "I told Sally to take Nan outside into the garden, and then I confronted Father. I really let him have it."

"When was this?" Jim asked, his tone steely.

Elaine hesitated. "Seventeen years ago," she said finally. "Sally's twenty-six now, so it must have been when she was about nine. I confronted him the same day she told me."

"And Mum didn't know?" I asked sharply. "You didn't tell her?"

"No," Elaine admitted quietly. "Mum didn't find out until years later."

A heavy silence filled the room, thick with unspoken accusations.

Jim broke the silence first. "Sally's reaction was understandable. She didn't know how to cope. How could she? But at least you had each other. Do you understand what it's like to survive alone? To carry that trauma without anyone to share it with?"

Elaine looked down, tears filling her eyes. "I was lucky," she whispered. "Lucky she told me early, lucky I could act on it. But that doesn't erase my guilt. I put her in that situation. It was my fault."

"Yes, it was," I said, my voice sharp and unforgiving. "It was your fault, Elaine. You knew exactly what he was capable of, yet you still left her there."

"I didn't think," Elaine said, her voice breaking. "I didn't believe it could happen again. I thought it was all behind us."

"Well, you thought wrong," I snapped, my anger rising to the surface. "You were wrong, and Sally paid the price. Just like I did. And even after you found out, you still sent her back there?"

"I know," Elaine whispered, tears now streaming down her face. "I know, April."

I was aghast. For seven more years, Elaine continued sending Sally back to stay with Mother and Father, even after discovering what had happened to her own daughter, Sally. It was incomprehensible, yet disturbingly familiar. Just like our mother had done with me, Elaine placed her daughter right back into harm's way, believing it enough to instruct Sally to stick close to Mum, as though proximity alone could keep her safe. I recognised that strategy immediately; I'd lived it myself, clinging close, carefully calculating every move, always hoping it would be enough to avoid the worst.

Mother, in her usual oblivious way, casually remarked how she'd always looked after Sally. Elaine's voice cut sharply through the air.

"He used to take any opportunity to abuse her," she said, her voice trembling but firm. "You only had to leave the room for a few minutes, Mum – just go to the toilet – and he'd pounce."

Her words hung heavily in the room, echoing painfully in my own memories. They were the exact words I'd struggled to find for years, raw and undeniable. I glanced at Mother, waiting for some reaction, a flicker of recognition. But there was nothing. Just the same blank expression, the same refusal to truly see.

173

Jim, who had been quiet until now, leaned forward, his voice cutting through the tension. "Do you understand what Sally's going through, Elaine? She's experiencing exactly what April went through, the fear, the silence, the overwhelming powerlessness."

He continued, turning toward the notes I'd kept close as reminders. "April's been writing things down," he said firmly. "One thing she wrote, something that feels very true, is that no one reached out to her for eleven years because deep down, they didn't want her around. They didn't want her talking, didn't want her telling the truth. Elaine's own admission confirms that. She just said herself, it suited her that April wasn't around during those eleven years."

"If I could go back," she said softly, "I'd change everything. But I can't. I can only try to make things right now."

Her words hung fragile and uncertain in the air. In that moment, a painful truth hit me again: there was no "making this right". There was only dealing with the wreckage left behind, clinging to a faint hope we might survive the aftermath.

Jim finally broke the silence. "Who else knows? Who has Sally told?"

Elaine shifted uneasily, eyes dropping to the floor. "I honestly don't know if she's told anyone," she admitted quietly. "Probably not. If she had... Frank would've ended up in prison, or worse."

"That's exactly what I faced," I said tightly.

Elaine glanced up briefly but quickly looked down again. Her next words were barely a whisper. "I can't change what happened."

My frustration boiled over. "But you still don't get it! Imagine yourself in my shoes. What if I'd slipped up and accidentally said something to Sally? How was I supposed to handle that? If I'd told her the truth, then what? How would I have lived with myself?"

My voice shook as I continued. "And the worst part is, I didn't even know it happened to her. I kept quiet to protect your relationship with her, but it turns out you managed to ruin that all on your own."

Elaine's expression crumpled, but she pushed forward, desperate. "I've been trying to figure out exactly when it started… when it all happened."

"Do you think it even matters?" I shot back bitterly. "Here's what matters: I wish to God I'd spoken to her. I wish I'd said something when I had the chance. But I didn't."

"Sally's done so much counselling, April. So much," Elaine murmured. "Yet I avoided talking about it for years, just like Mum avoided confronting Dad. Only recently have I begun to acknowledge it."

Elaine's face twisted with guilt. "I protected Mum instead of Sally. I should've gone to the police immediately, but I didn't. Instead, I told Sally, 'Mum's getting older, don't say anything.' I know now that I was wrong."

"Your relationship with your daughter should've been your priority," Jim said sharply.

"Don't you think I know that?" Elaine's voice cracked.

175

She sighed deeply, regret etched into her features. "Mum only found out recently, about a year and a half ago, maybe two years. Frank tried to touch Sally again, and when she told me, I completely lost it. I called him, screaming down the phone, 'Keep your filthy hands off my daughter!' I didn't know Mum had the phone on loudspeaker. She heard everything. Later, Elaine and Mother spent two hours demanding the truth, and eventually, he confessed."

It was only then, finally, that Mother accepted the truth of what he'd done.

Elaine paused, her voice tight, before quickly adding, "Yes, Sally found out Mum knew, because I told her. I don't even know why I did; it just slipped out. Ever since then, things have been strained."

Elaine looked away, her voice dropping lower. "And Sally, well… she's struggling now. She has real issues with Mum."

"Because she knows Mum was aware he'd done it before," I finished bitterly. "And she's right to feel that way."

My anger mingled with exhaustion as I stared at Elaine. "Yet, even knowing that, you didn't go to the police. You didn't stop him."

"No," Elaine admitted quietly. "I didn't. I was worried about what it would do to Mum, to Sally, and yes, even to me. And I regret that every day, April. More than you'll ever understand."

To me, Elaine had never seemed frightened or intimidated by him, so why would that suddenly change? Together, we'd had everything we needed to hold him accountable. But in my eyes, she chose to keep benefiting financially, letting

Sally suffer instead. It felt like Elaine was continuing exactly as she always had, only worse since she'd known about me.

For someone with her credentials and background, she'd spent an awful lot of time avoiding reality. Her occasional displays of guilt meant nothing to me now. Maybe she'd paid a price for her choices, but in my eyes, no more than she deserved.

This wasn't a mother teaching her daughter about right and wrong. It was a mother showing her daughter that money mattered more than anything else.

Her words carried genuine pain and regret, and although I wanted desperately to believe her, to find some shred of comfort, I knew it wasn't enough. It never would be.

Elaine hesitated, her voice faltering. "So what's the outcome here, April? Can we ever put this right?"

I shook my head slowly, exhaustion heavy in my voice. "No, Elaine. We can't just 'put it right'. It doesn't work like that. We have to work through it, bit by bit. That's the only way."

Elaine dropped her gaze to her lap, murmuring quietly, "Sally sees Mum as someone who should have protected her, and she's right."

I couldn't stop myself. "She is right. I had exactly the same issue with Mum. Exactly the same, Elaine. It's not just Sally."

Elaine shifted uncomfortably, her voice becoming defensive. "I know. I've counselled enough people to understand now, better than ever before, but… God, April, I was trying to protect Mum. Even then, it was always Mum."

Her words hit me hard. "You protected Mum? You put Mum above your own daughter? Elaine, you kept the truth hidden from me and from Sally. And for what? To spare Mum's feelings? Can you even hear yourself?"

"Yes," Elaine whispered, tears filling her eyes. "And I've paid for it. Every single day."

The conversation turned to Sally's pregnancy. "She's having a girl, you know," Elaine said softly, her voice full of sadness. "I think that's making everything worse. She's feeling protective in a way she never has before, and it's bringing it all back, every painful memory."

"I've been there, and I've worn the t-shirt twice," I said bitterly. "That's exactly how it should've been for you when Sally was born, Elaine!"

"And you're proud of Sally's strength now?" Jim cut in sharply. "Because that strength has come at a heavy price. A price she should never have had to pay."

Elaine nodded slowly, tears falling freely. "I know. But maybe there's something good in that strength. She's finally able to speak up, to acknowledge what happened. That counts for something, doesn't it?"

Her voice cracked as she continued. "I didn't truly understand what you went through, April, not until it happened to Sally. Only then did I fully grasp the weight of it."

There it was. Elaine laying bare exactly how little I had mattered to her.

"And now you have to live with that," I said coldly. "Just as I've had to live with it, just as Sally will have to live with it. That's your legacy, Elaine. Pain, silence, regret."

A heavy silence fell over the room. Elaine wiped her face and rose slowly. "I've got to go," she said quietly.

She quickly changed the subject, her voice wavering. "You've got your hospital appointment tomorrow, Mum, don't forget. And remember the dinner in the fridge."

Mum, distracted, shifted in her seat. "I've got so much going on tomorrow," she mumbled, adding the weight of the conversation to her mental list of burdens.

Elaine left, leaving Jim, Mum, and me in awkward silence.

I leaned forward, redirecting Mother's attention to the letters. "Do you remember asking me about these letters, Mum? The ones you and I exchanged?"

I pressed on gently. "You said something important to me the other week. You told me if you had these letters, the ones we wrote eleven years ago, and could read them again, you'd finally understand. And you'd finally be sorry. Sorry for everything."

Mum's voice broke, showing rare vulnerability. "I am sorry, April. For all the wasted years, for everything left unsaid. It was stupid. Both you and Elaine, fighting all these years over one bloody thing."

I shook my head firmly. "It wasn't just one thing, Mum. It started there, but it grew into something much bigger. It's about everything that happened afterward. All of you spent years hiding from the truth."

I handed Mum the letters carefully. "Read them," I said softly. "Take your time, read them properly. Maybe then we can finally start moving forward."

Mum nodded weakly, barely whispering, "I will. I promise."

We gathered our things to leave, the atmosphere unchanged, still heavy with everything unsaid. Mum clutched the letters but didn't look at them. "I'll read them later," she murmured, distant, already overwhelmed by their contents.

I nodded, though part of me doubted it would happen. Deep scars don't heal simply because someone reads a few words on paper. They remain, shaping everything without us even noticing.

There was no resolution, no neat ending. Maybe there never would be.

CHAPTER TWENTY-TWO

When Mother's Mask Slips

No sooner had I walked through the door than Mother remarked, "Another nice jumper you've got there," and she chuckled softly. "You're like that woman, oh, I can't think of her name. She had forty jumpers and still bought another whenever she went out."

There was a hint of jealousy in her voice, something new to me. Maybe seeing me less dependent on her money unsettled her, disrupted whatever plans or expectations she had. Her tone reminded me of the recent comment: "Big family, big house, big money!" It stung then, and it stung again now.

The conversation turned to Sally and her boyfriends, one even a policeman. Mum laughed about how Sally casually ended relationships, simply telling her, "I don't see him anymore, Nan," before quickly moving on to someone else. Mum seemed amused, even impressed, saying, "She's always been the boss in any relationship."

It struck me how involved Mother seemed in Sally's life, especially since Sally would soon tell us something quite different, blaming Nan for not protecting her properly when she was younger. I wondered who was telling the truth.

Mother then casually mentioned that she, Sally, Paul, Elaine, and Penny were going out for dinner that evening to celebrate Sally's birthday. Her tone was light, as if it was nothing special, yet I felt a flicker of hope. It seemed like the perfect chance for us to reconnect, but it quickly became clear there was no invitation for me. Subtle, yet painfully obvious; I wasn't welcome.

I mentioned another house on her road that had burnt down about a year earlier. Her expression tightened immediately. "And how do you know about that?" she asked sharply, suspicion in her voice.

I admitted honestly that sometimes I checked online to see if anything had happened near her. It felt human, a way of connecting when distance made everything else impossible.

"A phone call would've told you," she replied dubiously, clearly questioning more than my methods.

I cautiously countered, "Do you want to go there?" I hadn't expected her to engage, but surprisingly she muttered grudgingly, "We've got to go there sometime." The words felt strange, given her long-standing avoidance of the topic.

Before this visit, I carefully prepared copies of the six letters previously exchanged, stapled in the order sent. With four different highlighters, I marked key patterns and connections clearly, aiming to show exactly how each letter related to the next.

I laid out the letters carefully, explaining their sequence. None were dated, but the flow was obvious enough. Starting with the first letter, I highlighted Mother's line in green: "She was put out because she didn't get a thank-you note from Emma for a cheque, and Elaine didn't either, when Emma got married." In my reply, I highlighted my response in green: "You tell me that you and Elaine didn't receive thank-you notes."

In that same reply letter, I highlighted another line in orange: "For many years, I played happy families." It felt weighty, something I'd buried for too long, now boldly marked in bright, undeniable orange.

Next was Mother's second letter, where she responded, "I did not realise you were playing happy families." I highlighted this in orange, directly connecting her words to mine.

Then came another moment in her second letter, marked in yellow. Mother wrote, "So I'm sending a cheque for Louise and one from Elaine too." The underlying bitterness was clear. She and Elaine initially decided to withhold Louise's cheque entirely because Emma hadn't sent thank-you notes for wedding gifts, despite the girls marrying just eight weeks apart. It was as if they'd convinced themselves punishing Louise made sense, somehow blaming her. Only after I pointed out the unfairness did they relent and send the cheques.

In my next reply, I highlighted in yellow: "Thank you for Louise's cheques, but unfortunately uncashable because they were written out wrong." In Mother's final letter, her opening line read, "Sorry about the cheques," which I highlighted as a rare, though unsatisfying, acknowledgement.

Further down, Mother wrote, "I do understand the problems we are having." I highlighted this in blue, and in my final reply, also highlighted in blue: "You do not understand the problems we are having."

At this point, Mother said casually, almost dismissively, "I read the letters when I get bored." Her words felt like a deliberate slap, reducing my carefully expressed feelings

183

and the effort behind them to mere entertainment. Clearly, I wasn't a priority.

Everything was laid out clearly, colour-coded and simple, yet Mother seemed determined to confuse it. She waved her hand dismissively, arguing, "I didn't send three letters," and mixing up the order as though the evidence wasn't there. She was determined to twist things, confuse the facts, and dodge accountability.

How could she deny sending three letters when her handwriting was right there? Logic didn't matter here. When I read aloud my explanation for Emma's missing thank-you card, her blunt response shocked me: "Sounds like something you would make up to me."

I was stunned. "Mum, when have I ever lied to you?" My voice was sharper than intended. She hesitated, cornered, before quietly admitting, "Never."

A small blessing, perhaps, but even that moment of clarity didn't last.

We were supposed to discuss the letters, but Mother quickly steered us off course. She abruptly brought up something unrelated: "I said I'd leave him if he did it again," she declared defiantly, as if recalling some forgotten strength.

I quietly but firmly reminded her, "You never did."

Her response hit like a punch to the gut. "*I didn't know if you were creeping upstairs to join him,*" she said.

I was floored, utterly stunned by her cruelty. Had she really just said that? I steadied myself, trying to stay calm.

I returned to the letters, saying as evenly as possible, "The proof is all here." But she instantly pivoted, repeating her familiar refrain. "You threw me out of the car!" It felt rehearsed, like a well-practiced deflection. When pressed further, she shifted again, insisting, "I wrote that I'd meet up with you in Brentwood."

"But Mother, read your own letters," I insisted, holding them up clearly. "What you're claiming isn't there."

I suspected she thought we'd somehow removed her words, an impossibility, of course. Jim stepped in, reading the final line from my last letter aloud: "Look forward to you getting in touch with some answers."

Mother's blunt response was, "That's what I couldn't do. The answers."

There it was, exactly as I'd thought. She refused to put anything incriminating on paper, preferring silence over truth. She'd said just a week ago, "If you could show me three letters I wrote, I'd be truly sorry." Yet, faced with those letters now, her promise meant nothing.

I wondered if Elaine had influenced her again, planting seeds of doubt and undermining any willingness to admit the truth. It wouldn't be the first time.

Mother revisited her tired old line: "I'd leave him if he does it again." Around and around, the same deflections.

She then tried another angle: "It was different when he did it to Sally," she said coolly. "Basically, he was impotent."

Her words hung harshly in the air, as if impotence somehow excused the crime. I couldn't believe what I was hearing.

185

Regarding me, she offered yet another excuse. "I said I'd leave him if he did it again," she admitted, "but I didn't promise." It was a loophole she'd always clung to, freeing herself from accountability.

Mother was a walking contradiction, each justification another painful slap. Her denial ran incredibly deep.

Eventually, the conversation shifted to the Will and the POA. Just last week, Mum gave us clear permission to discuss both with Elaine. Since then, Elaine had clearly intervened, blocking our access. Mum now flatly denied ever giving permission.

"Why would you want to see them?" she asked, hostility dripping from her voice.

I tried to remain steady. "You said I was an equal, so why shouldn't I see them?"

Her response cut deeply: "You were an equal, but not anymore. Penny has been more of a daughter than you."

Her words hurt, but worse was realising her willingness to lie repeatedly. She'd become skilled at rewriting reality to suit herself.

We chose not to fight further, trying instead to defuse the tension. "Leave it, Mum. Don't worry about it." But she wouldn't stop. She seemed to relish calling us liars, unwilling to drop the subject.

Then she fully unravelled, unleashing obscenities and accusations. Each venomous word underscored her deep denial. In her mind, everything was my fault. I was to blame for it all.

I gently reminded her, "It wasn't me who brought this up today. I was going to leave the letters for you, let you read them in your own time." But she'd insisted on diving back into the same painful subjects.

Before leaving, I tried to ease the tension, but Mum was determined to drag it out. Eventually, exasperated, I said, "If you want to carry on, carry on." And she did, relentlessly.

Finally, she concluded bitterly, "It just won't work, will it?"

In a brief pause, I quietly asked, almost hesitantly, "Do you want to see me next week?" I wasn't even sure why I was asking after all she'd said today. Yet she surprised me by replying, "Yes."

My final words were gentle, sincere: "Go and have a lovely evening."

Unexpectedly, she reached out for a hug. "I'm sorry about today," she whispered softly.

Caught completely off guard, I held her tightly. Maybe, just maybe, she'd realised something today. Yet beneath it all lingered the sharp hurt she'd caused, and the unsettling thought that this could be our last hug. I clung tightly, desperate for this fleeting moment of connection.

Reflecting later, I felt the sheer weight of her brutality. I needed space to process it all. Elaine's continued silence added another layer of tension. I couldn't shake the suspicion that her influence was behind Mum's cruelty today, like an ever-present shadow shaping Mother's behaviour.

CHAPTER TWENTY-THREE

By Hand to Mother and Letters to Family Members

Mum,

I had hoped we would find some common ground and understanding, but you refuse to do this. You treat what has happened to me like some sort of game that has a point scoring system.

I did not realise until recently that you could be such a liar!

I asked you if Sally knew about what happened to me. You replied, "I don't know," and yet you <u>did.</u>

I asked you, "Am I equal to Elaine?" You replied, "Of course you are." I'm obviously not.

You gave us permission to ask for copies of the POA and the Wills; a week later, you say you didn't.

You said, "You would leave him if he did it again." He did it again, you didn't leave him.

Lie, after lie, after lie.

You have got deflecting down to an art. If there is an awkward question you do not want to answer, out comes that broken record: "But you threw me out of the car." The way you say it, you would think I did it physically, but you and I know that isn't true, unless that is another lie you want to create?

You are fully aware that Jim made contact after the car incident. Yet you try to change this to "it wasn't me". It's pathetic. You didn't get back in touch because it suited you, him, and Elaine not to have me around. (Refer to the letter dated October 2010 in your bedroom, two years before the car incident; you can hear in that letter that you are pushing me away, even then). Just admit it. LET'S NOT FORGET – the car incident would never have come about if he hadn't done what he'd done to me in the first place and by you choosing to stand by him. And yet you continue to still try and blame me for the last 11 years.

I have been trying to work my way through what he, and YES, you have done to me and have only been met with hostility, lies, and distortions of the truth. Whatever happened to me being the victim? It's all about you, Elaine, and money.

You are now left with your only daughter. Something you and she have wanted all along, telling me how happy you were before I came back. Well done!! You have achieved your goal.

Just be sure to remember that you are not Elaine's first priority; that lies with your money. Your words, I quote: "Elaine did not know if we were dead or alive; she went straight and got the money first." Give Elaine her due; SHE HAS DONE A GOOD JOB ON YOU. Feeding you with all the necessary information that you like to hear. A bargain here and a bargain there, leaving you believing she's done it all in your best interest. Oh, what a fool you can be, Mother. All she is doing is leaving herself with more of your money when you pass. She controls you like a puppet on a string. I nearly said to her when she honoured us with her presence the other week, "I hope you are not going to charge us for this!" It's absolutely, diabolically laughable, if it wasn't so sad.

You had the golden opportunity to make amends with the daughter that truly loved you and who did nothing other than protect you for so many years, and you have blown it because, as always, you have your priorities in the wrong place.

I have never been interested in your money. I've only ever wanted you to take responsibility for all the wrong you have done to me, something money cannot buy.

And the straw that broke the camel's back: you accused me as a young child, not knowing any different (if I, as a young child, were the perpetrator). You said to me, and I quote, "I DIDN'T KNOW IF YOU WERE CREEPING UPSTAIRS TO JOIN HIM." What a vile and sick statement to make to a victim of incest and child sexual abuse.

I have never come across two people who are so toxic and evil. I am ashamed to call you family, and be rest assured, I never wish to have any association with you both ever again!!

You and Elaine deserve each other. TWO EVIL MOTHERS TOGETHER! Be happy!

Bye.

As for Elaine and Penny, they are Del Boy and Rodney straight out of *Only Fools and Horses*. *"Stick with me, Rodney, and this time next year, we'll be millionaires!"*

In Elaine's own words: *"I never banked on Mum living this long."*

Letter to Family Members

I mentioned these letters before at the very beginning of this book, a glimpse of what was to come. Now, after all I've shared, you understand why it had to be written and why it could say nothing less than the truth. You know enough to understand what drove me to this final act of honesty, to lay bare everything I had held back for so long. Now is the time to let you see what truly passed between my family and me, now that you know all the dark, painful details of what my father did and the silence that followed. I had desperately hoped that we could work things out quietly. After everything, I still clung to the hope that Mum and Elaine might finally admit the truth and, in some way, acknowledge it. I hadn't wanted it to come to this, this letter that would tell the family what I had been forced to keep silent for so long. But every attempt to find peace with them had been blocked by their greed, their ignorance, and a refusal to see past their own comforts. My hopes were slowly, painfully, eroded, leaving me with no choice but to write the truth in black and white. They had left me with this one, final option.

The cursor blinked back at me. I'd spent some time, not too much, shaping each sentence, knowing that once I sent it, there'd be no going back. It wasn't anger that drove me; it was simply the need to be heard, finally, by the extended family who had kept me on the sidelines of my own life. I read the words again, feeling the weight of each line as it sank in. The cursor continued to blink steadily, waiting. I'd gone over every word, weighed every sentence. This letter was years in the making, years of holding back, swallowing down words I'd never dared to speak. But I was done with silence. I was done being the only one carrying the weight of these truths. I scanned the letter one more time, allowing myself to absorb each line – memories that had finally made their way into words. I printed them out and placed each one carefully into an envelope with the addresses of the intended recipients. I paused slightly at the post box before dropping them in, knowing there was no going back from this point onwards.

"I was sexually abused by my biological father, Frank Humphreys, from the age of 5 to 14."

It felt surreal, seeing those years laid out so plainly, like reading someone else's story. But they were mine, undeniably mine, even if Mum and Elaine had refused to face them. I wasn't seeking pity or alliances; I'd waited long enough for that. All I wanted was to be seen, to be heard, even just for a moment. For too long, I had protected everyone else's comfort and illusions. Those years were mine, not his, and not the family's, who had chosen to look away. I just wanted my voice to matter.

"I am not looking for sympathy or a shoulder to cry on; I just want to have a voice after being suppressed for too many years. If you are interested, carry on reading and please form your own opinion."

This wasn't a plea for support or validation. I was sharing my truth because I deserved to. I wanted them to understand those years, how isolated I'd felt and how sure I was that no one would believe me.

"...this was the mid-1960s and early 70s with no internet, iPads or iPhone, no Childline or #MeToo

movement. In my case, when the school was made aware, they sent me home – yes, home – to the abuser – my father."

The memory lingered, a fleeting relief, then the crushing truth that I wasn't safe. The adults I was supposed to trust had looked away, leaving me trapped. Whether my family understood or not, I was telling them anyway.

"My reason for not speaking out before or going to the police? It was the fear of not being believed... If it had gone to court and he had 'won', I would not have been able to survive that outcome. The fear of what would happen to me once he got out of prison if he was justly convicted. I was a child not wanting to be responsible for the family splitting up."

Fear had been my prison, keeping me silent. I'd been terrified my family would deny the truth, and they did, covering up Sally's abuse, just as they had for years with me. I thought of Mum and the first time I tried to tell her.

"Jo, my mother, who I first tried to tell when I was 5 years old, didn't listen then, and she's still not listening now."

I thought of Mum, and her pulling up my long cotton socks during the first time I tried to tell her what Father was doing. When she had been dismissive, as if my "news" was nothing but a nuisance. The years that followed only deepened the silence; pretending was easier than facing the truth. Even when she *truly* learned the truth in my teens, she saw *herself* as the real victim. She stayed with him, choosing to protect her own secrets.

"Since finding out the truth when I was a teenager, she has always considered herself more of a victim than me. She chose to stay with him and protect him, even though he went

193

on and committed the crime again. I've spent my whole life protecting my mother from her shame, when she should have been protecting me."

Yet she *never* has.

"Ostracised by my immediate family, I have only returned to them on the 4th October 2023, given that Frank has passed away and I feel more comfortable to do so. I was looking for some recognition to the wrong that was done by me, only to be met with the same constant denial I have always had to deal with."

Reading it now, I felt both sorrow and anger. My mother should have been the one I could rely on, but I had carried her shame while she ignored mine. And Elaine, she had made her choice too.

"Elaine has taken full advantage of the situation her whole life for either materialistic or financial gain... When I reminded her what she said, she replied, 'Don't remember saying it, but sounds like something I would say.'"

She had brushed it aside, sidestepping responsibility as if it were just another of her quirks. Yet she knew; she had seen things that should have absolutely haunted her. Still, she chose to ignore it, even leaving her own daughter in the care of a man she knew was dangerous.

"Why did she allow our mother and father to look after her daughter Sally? Backed into a corner, Elaine revealed that he also sexually abused Sally between the ages of 7 and 9. She had no excuse for leaving her there; in fact, in one instance she attempted to blame me for it! At this point, she wholeheartedly, openly admitted taking full advantage of everything she possibly could from our parents.

Elaine didn't tell my Mum for 10 years and yet still allowed Sally to be looked after by them after she found out! Elaine has admitted she never told me, because she knew that at this point I would have gone to the police. Yes, she may have had to pay the price with her daughter's relationship, but if so, no more than she deserves, due to her constant lies and her ongoing greed."

My breath caught at her confession, Mum, Jim, and I listening as she stumbled over her words. She had known and still left her daughter in their care, even blaming me at one point. Now, as a counsellor, she ignored the very truths she once admitted: "Yes, I put my own daughter second."

"Did I mention her job? Elaine is a counsellor for sexual abuse victims. In the 13 years we have not seen each other, she could never find it in her heart to reach out and help me, her sister."

I read that line again, letting the hurt sink in. She had built her career on compassion for other victims, while never once extending that kindness to her own family. To me.

"You might ask, why am I speaking up now? The answer to that is I am done with possibly being seen in a worst light. Mum and Elaine never told me about the fire; people maybe noted my absence and no one truly knew why. I didn't have an interest in attending Frank's funeral. I must add, I wasn't told the date of the funeral, not that I wanted to attend, but because I obviously had no respect for Frank and could not sit there and hear nice things said about him. I only knew him as a 'monster'. You will have noticed Sally didn't attend the funeral either; Elaine arranged the funeral whilst Sally was on holiday – another cover up and lie.

All I've ever wanted out of all this is to be seen in a FAIRER light."

That last line was the heart of it. I wasn't asking for them to change the past, to take back their choices. I was simply asking to be seen, for my story to be acknowledged. Not hidden away, not ignored.

"He chose to sexually abuse me. My mother chose to stay with him. Elaine chose to take advantage of the situation. I had NO CHOICE."

It was my truth, laid bare. I couldn't change the past, couldn't erase their choices, but I could finally tell my story. Taking a deep breath, I posted my letters. I had no illusions that it would change anything, but I felt the weight of silence lift. This was my story, my voice, and now it was out there.

"Thank you for taking the time to read this, I would love to hear from you and if you do want to make contact, this is my email: april********@gmail.com. If you do not, I understand."

CHAPTER TWENTY-FOUR

Sally's Visit

In the early afternoon, I received an email from Elaine:

"Could you make yourself available around 4:30 pm today as Sally wants to come down and see you. She will be alone."

I decided not to respond. It was clear to me that Sally's visit was not well-intentioned. Furthermore, I was irritated by Elaine's presumptuousness. She seemed, in her normal arrogant manner, to expect us to just be at her beck and call after she had ignored all my previous emails. As we sat and waited, we could sense the simmering tension, knowing it likely stemmed from my decision to speak openly about everything that had happened at the hands of my father.

When I heard Jim's phone ring, which signified someone had pressed the button on our electric gates, I stayed put. Jim went out to meet her. From the start, Sally's voice carried a strained edge, her frustration evident as she approached. Yet, as their conversation unfolded, the initial anger softened, her words slowing, her tone calming.

When the storm seemed to have settled, I stepped outside and I spoke.

"I'm sorry, Sally, but it was not an easy decision to make to include you in my story, but, I'm afraid, through no fault of my own, your story became entwined in mine. I know you're starting a new life, and I didn't mean for my story to spill over into yours. But you are part of it, and it's difficult to separate our past from everything I'm trying to put into words now."

The atmosphere remained slightly taut, but now with a sense of tentative peace. Jim broke the silence, his voice calm yet pointed. "How can we help you?"

"Would you like to come in?" I offered gently.

Sally took a deep breath, her hands instinctively cradling her belly. "Not right now. I'm feeling quite shaky," she admitted, "I'm heavily pregnant..." Her partner Paul was with her, standing in the background, there to support her if need be.

Jim nodded. "Well, we're here now, so what's on your mind?"

She hesitated, her voice faltering. "I've heard things, information I wasn't comfortable with being shared."

Jim glanced at me, his jaw tightening. "Look, April's been through enough already. Our whole family's had enough." His gaze held steady as he added, "April has every right to tell her story."

Sally pressed her hands a bit tighter against her belly. "But I don't want my story mixed in. I'm not ready... I don't even know how it's affected me. I'm just starting this new life."

I looked at her, my voice soft but resolute. "Believe me, it wasn't easy, Sally. I know you've had your own pain, but after years of silence, I had to find my voice. Sally, it was not an easy decision. I know you're a victim as well as I am, but it was taken out my hands by your mother and your nan.

I thought, when your grandad died, they might have shown some remorse and understanding. That's all they had to do."

Sally looked down. "I get it. I'll tell you something. I've heard about your visits and the emails, and I've seen them, and each and every time I have actually been on your side. I understand that we've both got different stories. I completely get that, and I know that you've been going through this so much longer than me. I just did not want my name brought up. I was more than happy for you to tell your story. I'm actually so happy that you feel like you can do that now and tell your family. But I wanted to start fresh… free of all this."

"Let's go inside," I said. She looked at me, her expression softened and weary. "Can I have a hug?" I asked. After all, here was my niece, whom I'd had quite a lot to do with when she was a child; I just wanted to embrace her for more reasons than one. One thing it was not for, though, was guilt.

She nodded, and I wrapped her in a hug that felt both fragile and grounding. Her boyfriend looked at me expectantly. "Could I have one too?" he asked, smiling slightly. I gave him a quick hug, and together, we all walked into the house.

A quietness filled the room, each person lost in their own thoughts. Jim's voice broke the silence, gentle but firm. "Sometimes, telling your story is the only way to take control. April found that out the hard way. I think part of what you've got to remember is, as much as that's your story, April has a story too, which your mum happily tells Penny, and she tells you, without speaking to April first."

Sally nodded, processing it all. "You know, April, as soon as I found out that he sexually abused you too, I had a mental breakdown. I just... I need space to live my story, too. Without everything attached. I'm not siding with my mum or my nan. I know you haven't had their support in many years."

The room fell silent again.

The conversation took on a more sombre note as Jim, his voice steady but raw, leaned forward, looking Sally directly in the eyes. "You need to understand, Sally," he started, "I've been at this with April for 43 years. The weight of it all... it doesn't fade. I thought when we first spoke to your mum, she understood and saw things clearly. But then she started accusing April and blaming others, anyone but herself. It was as if, by blaming others, she thought she could keep the truth at bay. It doesn't work like that. April's had no choice. She had to keep away from the family. When Frank was still alive, she was scared of him, as you probably know; she couldn't be in same room as him. Now, April is trying to get her family back. The only way to get her family back is to tell her story. And unfortunately, you're part of that, and that's just unfortunate. Your mum blamed April for leaving you with Frank," said Jim.

I continued. "I never left you there, your mum did. I was never asked to look after you – your nan was. We never even left our own girls with him! If I was aware you were being left alone with him, I would have definitely removed you from the situation."

Sally said, "I appreciate that, I do, and I think it's twisted. Trust me, I've had so many arguments with my mum about it. I feel like, if anyone's going to understand you, it's

200

probably me, because they haven't had to endure what we did."

Also, as far as Sally was concerned, "Nan knew before Elaine told her."

I nodded, my fingers interlaced tightly as I leaned into the memories, acknowledging the burden I'd carried alone for years. I glanced at Sally, sensing the pain mirrored in my niece's eyes. "I never wanted this to spill over to you, Sally. It's not an easy thing to understand, and I know you're part of it now, whether you wanted to be or not. But this," – my voice faltered – "it's the only way I could make peace with what happened. I've not been heard or believed for so long, and the full, honest story needed to be said."

Sally, shifting slightly in her seat, let out a deep breath, her hands cradling her pregnant belly protectively. "It's... hard. Knowing my name is tangled up in all of this. It's been months, and I haven't told a soul about any of this... not my in-laws, not anyone. I didn't want to drag them into our family's history."

"Yes," I said, "but you have no idea what *I* have had to endure. Do you know what your nan said to me last week? She said, 'I didn't know if you were creeping up the stairs to join him.' What a sick thing to say, to a victim of sexual abuse. Also, your mum has blamed me for what happened to you. I will never understand that."

Sally interrupted. "Look, I may know why that is. I wanted to tell you about the situation. I remember one occasion when you were round with Nan. I remember sitting on the chair and I was begging to go. And, like you said in that email, everyone has their own memory, so I'm not judging that at all. But for me, and in my memory, as

201

soon as you walked out that door, it happened. He abused me. And so that's a memory that is screwed into my brain, and you are there, burned into that memory. And, for years, which I didn't realise until later on, I was questioning myself, wondering why you had left me there. It was me that questioned it. And then I found out about what happened to you, and everything in my mind went crazy."

"I appreciate what you believe to be your memories," I said, "but I can assure you again that if I had ever seen you alone in his company, I would never have left you there." And your mum knew what he'd done to me, and yet *she* left you there!

Sally said. "I want you to know I never meant to hurt you or make you feel that way. When I questioned things earlier, it was more of an internal thought process – something I was grappling with myself. For example, when Nan's house burned down, I briefly considered contacting you, April, but it didn't feel right at the time. Through it all, I've been thinking of you and hoping things would get better. But my mum, she just doesn't understand, because she hasn't been through it like us."

"And with your mum, it's different. She took advantage of the situation, used my misfortune to her benefit. She admitted as much. It's always been about money and what she can get out of people, including you. I know she's your mum, but you need to see her actions for what they truly are."

Jim nodded, his voice softening. "That's the thing, love. People who haven't lived it, they don't get it. They laugh, they joke, they move on... But for you, for April, it's stitched into every part of your life." He glanced briefly at me, then back to Sally, his eyes kind. "When April and I married, I promised to stand by her. But even then, I never knew how much this would be part of our lives… how much it would take out of her to finally face it."

I took a shaky breath, my voice almost a whisper. "The hardest part was that… it didn't end when I left home. Even after he died, the memories… they followed me, followed Jim and me through every chapter. And I'd hoped, really, truly hoped, that Mum would one day just acknowledge what happened. But she was too stubborn."

Sally chimed in, "It's so frustrating, April. I finally built a new life away from them, away from all the hurt. I moved to escape that situation, and just when I thought I was free, everything gets stirred up again. It's exhausting. I just want to leave it all behind and finally have some peace." Sally looked very serious. "I know how much this has cost you, Mum's… Mum's different, too, now. But the past doesn't disappear just because we ignore it. I'm giving birth next week, and I wanted to make a fresh start. I wanted to be free of it." Her voice cracked, eyes brimming with tears. "But here it is, again."

Jim spoke. "You've got your own family to think about now. Your baby. This little one will be a fresh start, a chance for you to make things different. But… don't think we don't understand. This will be your chance to find strength in it."

I nodded gently, echoing Jim's sentiment. "You're stronger than you know, Sally. You're starting a family, building something new. Let this be your new beginning. But know… if you ever need to talk, if you ever need to understand, I'm here. Jim's here."

Sally wiped a tear away, steadying herself. "I know. And I'm grateful. I just… I wish things could've been different. What bothers me most is how he seems to have gotten away with it – because he died without being blamed. It's like a constant weight, a reminder of the injustice. I see it happening again with this guy at work – he takes advantage and faces no consequences. It's a trigger, a reminder of my own experience, and it makes me furious."

Although I agreed with Sally, I, more than anyone, get a great deal of joy at the thought of that evil, sick bastard not existing anymore. My whole body eases just knowing he has been wiped from this planet, now rots in hell, and can do no more harm to anybody.

"Sally, I wanted to tell the police so badly, but I was terrified of not being believed. That fear was confirmed when I realised my own mum didn't want me to tell the police. It's devastating to go through abuse, but to then be dismissed or doubted adds another layer of trauma. The thought of your mum and nan denying it to protect him was unbearable."

Sally's gaze drifted out the window, her voice soft as she spoke. "I always wondered… if it was just me who felt invisible, unheard. Growing up, I had this… this sense of not being seen. Mum was there, but she wasn't, you know?"

Jim looked at her, nodding slowly, a quiet understanding in his eyes. "You weren't alone in that, Sally. That feeling… it's part of what April has carried for years. It's… it's what happens when truth gets buried, when nobody wants to look at what's right in front of them." His voice was steady, but there was an edge of sorrow that he couldn't quite hide.

I said, "I tried so hard to protect you from all of this, Sally. But I see now… maybe by keeping it all so hidden, I left you in the dark, too, and I'm sorry for that. I truly am."

Sally swallowed, her throat tight. "I don't blame you, April. I think I always knew that there was more going on than anyone was saying. And maybe that's why I wanted so desperately to know… to understand, even if it hurts."

Jim's eyes softened as he watched Sally, her bravery stirring a deep admiration in him. "You have every right to know, Sally. And if understanding this helps you… even a little, then it's worth it. Because you deserve to break free of it, to start your own family without carrying the weight of the past."

I looked up, meeting Sally's gaze with a fierce protectiveness. "You're not going to live in the dark like we did, Sally. I'll make sure of it. Whatever you need to know, whatever questions you have… I'm here to answer them, to make it as clear as I can."

Sally nodded, her voice barely a whisper. "Thank you. I just… I need to know why. Why didn't anyone… say something sooner?"

Jim let out a heavy sigh, running a hand over his face. "Sometimes, love, people think that by staying quiet, they're protecting those they love. But silence… it doesn't protect, not really. It just grows heavier, until it's too much to carry." He glanced at me, a knowing look passing between us. "But we're here now. We're here to help you carry it, to make sure you're not alone in this."

A small smile crossed Sally's lips as she looked between us. "I'm so grateful… to have you both here, to finally understand what was always just… hidden in the shadows."

My eyes filled with a mixture of pride and sadness. "You're brave, Sally. Braver than any of us were back then. And you're going to build something beautiful out of all this. I know it. I know you're going through a tough time, and I don't want you to suffer in silence like I did. Find your strength within. It won't be easy; life throws all sorts of challenges our way, things we think we can't handle. But we find a way, we persevere, and we grow stronger. This baby will bring new responsibilities. You'll find a way to make it work, just like you've always done."

I took a deep breath, letting my own words sink in, taking heed of my own advice. There was a new resolve in Sally's eyes, a spark of strength that seemed to grow as she spoke. "I don't want to carry bitterness, April. I don't want to spend my life feeling angry at things I can't change." She looked at Jim, her gaze steady. "But I do want to understand, so I can let it go... so I can be free of it."

Jim nodded, his voice gentle yet unwavering. "That's all anyone can hope for, love. To understand enough to let go." He paused, choosing his words carefully. "But it's also okay to feel angry sometimes. You've every right to feel the things you feel."

I leaned in closer, my expression softening. "Jim is right, Sally. It's not wrong to feel it. The hurt, the anger, it's part of healing. I had to face a lot of it myself, and it took years." I gave Sally a small, encouraging smile. "But you have something we didn't: a chance to talk about it together, out in the open. We're here to walk with you through it."

Sally looked between the two of us and said, "I think that's what I've needed all along... to feel like I'm not alone in this."

Jim said, "You have that now, Sally. Whatever's happened, whatever's been buried, none of it changes that. You're part of us. Always have been."

I continued. "And we see you, Sally. All of you. Your strength, your kindness, even the parts that hurt. That's what family's supposed to be, isn't it? Seeing each other through everything, no matter how messy."

Sally nodded, her own eyes misting over. "Thank you, both of you. For being here now, even if… even if it took so long."

The room fell quiet, a peaceful kind of silence settling in as we sat together, bound by unspoken understanding.

After a moment, Jim broke the silence, his voice warm yet firm. "Now, if there's anything you want to ask, anything at all, we're here to answer. No more shadows, no more silence."

Sally took a steadying breath, feeling the weight of all the questions she'd carried for so long. "I just… I want to know what happened. To you, April. Why it all became… like this."

I took a deep breath, my voice barely above a whisper. "There are things that happened… things I wish hadn't. But it was the silence, the pretending. What he did was horrific, but what your mum and nan did hurt just as much." I paused, gathering my thoughts. "I was taught not to question, not to speak. But that silence… it grew into something that poisoned everything."

Jim reached over, his hand resting on mine, grounding me. "And we've lived in that silence for too long, but now April is speaking out."

"You might not think I've done you any favours now," I said, "but you will in the long run." I asked her to let me know when the baby arrived and to tell me her name, to which she agreed.

Sally looked at us, a quiet determination in her eyes.

"I've needed this, really. But I have to go now. Thank you."

"We're here," I said.

"I know that now, thank you. Look, Merry Christmas."

"Merry Christmas, Sally."

And she left.

CHAPTER TWENTY-FIVE

After Sally's Visit

Afterwards, I couldn't shake the sense that Sally's experiences and feelings seemed to mirror mine. It was strange how even our words had a way of reflecting each other's. I wanted to trust her, to believe that maybe things were finally heading somewhere, but something in me resisted. My instincts screamed at me that this would be the one and only time I'd see her.

We knew Sally's baby was due mid-December, a planned C-section. But as predicted, we heard nothing. Sally, like her mother, only reached out when there was something in it for her.

On the 18th January 2024, Jim took our statements, his and mine, and handed them directly to my mother. Elaine happened to be there, saw the letters, and without a moment's hesitation, shared the contents with Sally. Naturally, Sally didn't take kindly to parts of what we had written.

Emails started to fly over from Sally in the following days. In one, Sally told us that she had reported Jim and myself to the police for harassment, citing the statements we'd given to my mother and Elaine. Sally even claimed that Jim had told her, "We didn't want anything to do with her." A complete and utter lie.

The irony wasn't lost on me. After all, the ones who had truly harmed, who had covered up the abuse, had never faced justice. But a few paragraphs from us, that was enough to bring out accusations and threats.

Eventually, Sally sent what we believed to be her final email. It read, "This email is to let you know I no longer intend to go back and forth with yourself. It is too traumatic." I replied, agreeing it had been difficult for us both and reminding her that I'd only responded to her emails. I also added, "It saddens me that you do not want to keep in touch. My door is always open to you."

In the end it was the contents of those statements that caught Elaine's attention. Until then, she'd largely ignored me, pretending her own actions were somehow invisible. But seeing everything laid out plainly in black and white forced her to face the things she'd long dismissed. I could tell she thought sending Sally in first might soften me. But I wasn't taken in. I saw right through her motives and held my ground.

Despite the tensions, Mother and Elaine agreed to meet on the 26th of February 2024. Back in November, Mother had spitefully told me that while I was still in their Will, I was no longer an equal beneficiary. They had many times assured me through the years that it would be a 50/50 split. Naturally, I felt wronged.

Later, I discovered that their Will had been changed in 2016. That day, we discussed many things, and then out of the blue, Elaine offered to adjust things to make sure I received a larger share.

For the first time in a long time, I felt a glimmer of hope. Though my mother couldn't understand me, maybe Elaine did, at least a little. I didn't care about the money itself, but the fact that Elaine acknowledged the unfairness, that she saw my side, meant something.

The next day, 27th February, I received an email from Sally. She mentioned she'd spoken to the police and asked them not to pursue her complaint. This struck me as odd. It had been six weeks since she'd reported us, and we hadn't heard a thing. Sally added that she was glad to hear that we were handling things "in a civil manner" now. Sally was seeing it as a "given" now money was on the table.

I was left feeling unsettled. It seemed like progress, but where it went from here was still largely down to her mother and mine. So many questions still remained unanswered. I told Sally as much in my response, letting her know that if the police wanted to speak with us, they were still welcome. We still had nothing to hide.

On the 2nd of March 2024, Elaine's email landed in my inbox. "As I said on the 26th of February, I am willing to address a percentage of Mother's estate to be given to April. An agreement can be written up within a couple of weeks, on the condition that there is no more talk about Elaine, Mother or Sally." And there it was. Elaine had led me to believe that, finally, she understood, that maybe she even cared. But this was just another attempt to silence me, just as they had done my whole life. No mention of a non-disclosure agreement had come up during our meeting in February, yet here it was, Elaine's solution, as always: get out the cheque book to solve the problem.

The most infuriating part was that I'd spent the last six months pouring out emails, explaining how, now that Father was gone, it was the first time I could finally speak openly about what happened. What had been glaringly clear, though, was that Sally, just like her mother, assumed money would be the answer, because, for her, it always had been.

211

This was the piece of the puzzle that had been staring me in the face when my instincts kicked in and screamed at me that I would see Sally only once. Proving to be just like her mother – it all came back to money. Sally had assumed I'd be kept in line with money too. That's why she called off the police; she saw it as a given that I'd do what she did, be paid off and stay silent.

We had arranged to meet Mother and Elaine on the 24th of March 2024. The day was filled with tense discussion. Mother and Elaine were as belligerent as ever. Eventually, it became too much to bear, so I decided to step out, get some fresh air and walk up the road to clear my head.

To my surprise, or maybe not entirely, as I walked along, I spotted Sally, Paul, their baby and a puppy in the distance. It would have been too obvious if they'd turned and walked away, and I wasn't about to do the same either. So, before I knew it, we found ourselves face to face. I prepared for the polite exchange of "hellos" and nothing more. Sally had her baby wrapped up in a sling, and I instinctively leaned in to get a closer look.

What happened next took me aback. As I moved in, Sally pulled her baby back, almost as if I were a threat to her. I was flabbergasted. What had I done to deserve that? I quickly stroked the puppy and then excused myself, saying I'd only come out to get some air.

When I returned to the bungalow, I casually mentioned, "Guess who I just bumped into. Sally!" Elaine's reaction was instant. "We should invite Sally in and let her have her say."

She was clearly hoping to deal with the old April. If Sally and the baby came in, she thought it might soften me enough to get me to sign the non-disclosure agreement (NDA). But I wasn't falling for it. It was no coincidence that Sally had appeared; this meeting was clearly orchestrated.

How could I express anything real when there was a baby and a puppy in the room, clearly meant to disarm me? We had serious matters to address with Mother and Elaine, but once again, Elaine was pulling her strings, using every tool she could find. Her manipulation knew no bounds.

As we continued, we started pressing Elaine with questions. Each answer, however, was either an "I don't know" or "I can't remember", as if she was stuck in a loop. Finally, I could not hold back and told her that she sounded just like one of those guilty criminals who sits in an interview room, repeatedly saying "no comment" to every question on tape. It was maddening.

One of her evasive "don't know" answers came when we asked her how much she had withdrawn from Mother's bank account before the fire. Eventually, we got a real answer. Our question: Have you or Penny received any money since Frank's death? Elaine replied with a blunt "Yes."

"Was it a gift or wages?" I asked.

"I don't know," she muttered.

"And what about Sally?" I pressed.

"Yes, Sally was gifted some money."

"How much?"

Elaine's face twisted as she snapped, "Why do you need to know? What difference does it make if it was £1,000 or £50,000? And Penny and I got back pay for work on the bungalow."

And there it was, laid bare. They'd bought Sally and Penny's silence. We'd seen a piece of paper in Mother's rented place, written in Elaine's handwriting, which read "£25,000 to Sally, £25,000 to Penny". After Elaine's cagey comment about amounts, it felt fair to assume they had indeed received £25,000 each.

This was Elaine at her most manipulative. Since the fire, she had been telling anyone who would listen, friends, neighbours, cousins, and even local businesses, that Mother and Father were not insured. Whilst this was true, what she likely never revealed was that it was not a mistake. It was a deliberate choice they had made years ago to stop paying the insurance.

In response, people rallied to help. Cousins, friends and neighbours came from far and wide, some giving a day's free labour. Others working for weeks without payment. Local businesses offered discounted materials, and the bungalow slowly got rebuilt. They were showered with generosity, clothing, bedding still in their packaging, a brand-new television gifted for free. A local store even started a fundraising page, probably under the impression that Mother and Father couldn't afford the cost of a rebuild.

But once the dust had settled and Mother was back in her home, Elaine made her move. She convinced Mother to gift thousands upon thousands of pounds to Sally and Penny, calling it "back pay" for work done on the bungalow. There was no thought for the countless people who had selflessly helped, nor any consideration for Mother's future care costs.

When I walked away from Mother in November 2023, I am sure they thought it would be for good and that's when the money got dished out. They did not envisage me showing up again.

CHAPTER TWENTY-SIX

Jim's Statement

Jim has always been the kind of person who supports quietly from the sidelines, not one to make a fuss or draw attention to himself. That's why it's so significant when he decides to express his thoughts and feelings in writing; it's not his usual way. He's always been my biggest supporter, my silent pillar of strength in the chaotic and gross whirlwind that my family life can sometimes be. So, when Jim actually sits down to write a letter like this, it speaks volumes about his deep commitment and the strength of his convictions.

Writing isn't something Jim does on a whim. He's the sort who thinks long and hard before he puts pen to paper, making sure his words carry the weight of his intentions. This letter is a rare insight into what he's been witnessing and feeling all these years, a side of him that even I don't see very often. It's a heartfelt outpouring from a man who typically shows his love through actions rather than words, making this letter all the more poignant and powerful.

It cannot have been easy…

For Jim to articulate his feelings and take a stand in such a public way shows just how much he cares and how determined he is to defend and support me. It's an act of loyalty and bravery that only makes me appreciate him more. Each word he wrote reinforced why I feel so fortunate every day to have him in my life. Here's Jim's letter, a true testament to his character and to the depths of his dedication to me. Reading through it, I hope you can understand the profound bond we share and why I consider myself incredibly lucky to call him my husband.

The Statement

Jo,

He forced his penis in her mouth on regular occasions from the age of 5 to 13. He made her watch porn and then did the same; he went into her room in the dark of night and ran his hands all over her whilst she cried and you told her to FORGET IT AND MOVE ON. HOW SICK ARE YOU?

She is now a 61-year-old woman I have known and loved for over 43 years who still has nightmares - nightmares, I have listened to her cry in her sleep on many occasions, saying, "No, no, please stop," but it's not the crying or words of a 20-, 30-, 40-, 50- or 60-year-old woman, it the crying of a 5, 6, 7, 8-year-old child and it still happens to this day. I lay there listening, helpless, because I know if I try to wake her up by touching her, it will literality make her jump out of the bed in fright, that my touch to her will make her think it's him all over again, so I lay there and listen until she usually wakes herself up and then eventually settles down and goes back to sleep,

I have witnessed for many years the self-harming she has done to herself, digging her nails into her thighs and legs and scratching her arms until they bleed. This when it all got too much for her and usually after visiting you where she tried to talk to you only to be shut down by you and with your constant denial and lack of understanding or compassion.

In her early 30s, she was drinking and smoking more than she was eating. Her weight was under 9 stone and she was falling into full depression. She went to the doctors, who put her in touch with a psychiatrist. He recommended that you, Frank and Elaine attend counselling sessions to help April. You, Frank and Elaine, the cowards you are, point-blank refused to help her.

When April was speaking to you and Elaine, she said, do you know where I would be without Jim? Elaine's blasé reply was, "You are going to say you would be dead," which was true. You said nothing, no reaction, no caring hug, no sorry you felt like that, nothing. Both you and Elaine must have ice running through your veins, not blood. And as for Elaine's reaction, let's hope she doesn't treat her paying clients with the same blasé attitude.

Since his death, she has been having dreams that he is in our house, sitting in the chair, waiting.

IT NEVER GOES AWAY OR CAN BE FORGOT ABOUT.

You recently criticised her for showing no interest in Terrance. April explained the reasons why to you and you just turned up your spiteful nose.

However, I had conversations with Frank, where he told me that you and him never expected April to look after Terrance. He told me that Elaine would be left an extra £15,000 in your Will(s) and this was to help her look after Terrance. He said you both knew April couldn't cope with the responsibility of looking after him. You accused her of never visiting him, which is true, but why not ask yourself this question: how many times did you tell April that you were going to visit Terrance, and would she like to come? The answer, from memory, was – NEVER.

With regards to April telling you to get out of the car, this was done because she tried to do something nice for you by picking you up and taking you to see your 1st great grandchild, but you decided that you wanted to speak about why you weren't allowed to go to Emma and Louise's weddings; you kept going on about how hurt you were. April didn't invite you to the weddings, to protect you from people that might know your business and want to confront you about it. Given the crime, not everyone, like April, would want to protect you.

April explained to you that she had already told you 18 months ago the reasons why and didn't want to go over it again. She was trying to do something nice for you, but you carried on; you wanted to talk about the past and April didn't. Here is the reason why April lost it with you.

You sitting there bleating on and talking about how hurt you were about something that happened to you 18 months ago, but when April wanted to talk to you about what happened to her 20, 30, 40 years ago, you refused to talk; you shut her down, you told her to move on. No wonder she lost it and told you to get out of the car. The sheer gall and double standards of you were and still stay unbelievable.

After this, April wrote/replied to you three times, Each time ending with asking you to keep in touch/contact. You never replied to her last letter. Despite this, April asked me to contact you. I contacted Elaine by email and phone to see how you were and you still made no contact.

We tried to make contact. YOU left it for 11 years and only made contact when Frank died and only because

Elaine said that you needed to let April know because of some legal form she had to fill in, otherwise you probably would never have made contact.

You have also been selective in telling the story about April not visiting you. Why haven't you told people how she used to come over and visit you every week, when he was out working or playing golf, 1 1/2 to 2-hour round trip in traffic to see you, until YOU decided that he would not leave the bungalow so she could visit? That didn't put April off; she would then come and pick you up, bring you to our house then take you back home, A total trip of over 3 1/2 to 4 hours in traffic to see her mum. So when you tell others your stories, tell them ALL the facts.

The truth is you never wanted her around you, as April was a constant reminder to you of what he and you had done; you never wanted to talk to April about what happened for the same selfish reasons; you never made contact in the last 11 years for the same reason.

As for Elaine, her so-called elder sister, she openly admitted in front of us that she took full advantage of April's and, more sickening, her own daughter's sexual abuse to gain as much financially as she could from him and you.

You and Elaine will both recall saying that April was not money oriented. This is true; she never has been. She has never been interested in your or his money, only trying to get your understanding of what he did and how it affected her. You also said she was never ambitious enough; more hurtful words from an unloving uncaring self-centred so-called mother.

You and Elaine probably expected that when April walked away in November, that was the last you would see and hear from her, that if you didn't make contact as you hadn't in the previous 11 years, that would be the end of it, but that's not going to happen this time.

You may soon receive a letter from our solicitors as we intend to sue both Frank's estate for historical child sexual abuse, emotional neglect, child neglect and emotional stress. This list is not exhaustive; in the event that you may pass away before this case goes to court, we intend to sue your estate with the same. Our solicitor will set out the full legal details in the letter to you and Elaine. This is just to let you know it's coming. Therefore, whoever is dealing with or has dealt with Frank's estate, you may need to let them know.

We intend to find Ted and Sally's addresses, and we will send them copies of all letters; they can then form their own opinions.

I will be writing to the person(s) who helped fundraise the money for you and to the shops that gave you discounted goods to help you rebuild your bungalow, to all your neighbours, to tell them what sort of people they helped. But don't worry yourselves; I only intend to tell them the truth.

We are also considering writing to Elaine's professional conduct team about how she has the front to advertise herself as a warm, caring counsellor whilst leaving her own sister to struggle, and to cover up her own daughter's sexual abuse is hypocritical beyond words.

This is not about financial gain, being spiteful or revenge; this is about justice for April for how all three of you have treated her over the last 56 years. You all have had plenty of opportunities to show some sort of remorse and more importantly to help April when she needed your help, but instead all 3 of you chose to bleat on about how it affected you as individuals, casting April and, yes, Sally aside in order to protect yourselves.

We had hoped we would be able to keep Sally out of all of this; however, that will be impossible, because once you, Elaine, left her with Frank to be sexually abused and when you decided to tell Sally about what happened to April without April's permission, YOU MADE Sally part of April's story. And this is April's story to tell to whom she wants. April has tried in vain to explain to you over many years all this and more is a consequence of what Frank and, yes, you, Jo, did to April.

Elaine said that she didn't know how he sexually abused Sally as she wouldn't tell her, but she does as she witnessed and watched Frank sexually abuse April; however, she now knows what he was capable of doing.

Jo, you may recall that you very spitefully and vindictively asked April "what were you protecting me from?" Well, you now have your answer. THIS!

Initially, Jim planned to write and send his statement without my knowledge, and I couldn't have blamed him. He's carried so much of this weight over the years. But he decided to tell me, and I was all for it. I've been in the background, doing nothing wrong, for far too long, and I decided to write a statement too.

CHAPTER TWENTY-SEVEN

My Statement

In the 11 years I didn't hear from you, I obviously didn't know how things would work out, but I always liked to convince myself that if he died first, you would express remorse and many apologies for every wrongdoing done to me in the past. How wrong could I be?

One thing that has been consistent with me until now is that I always gave you the benefit of the doubt and protected you in the process.

You, on the other hand, have maintained to see the worst in me, with no logical explanations to back up what you say, and as for you protecting me, that never entered your head for my entire life.

You were a 'pimp'. You made me do the job you were supposed to do as his wife.

An overall reflection of my childhood – I can honestly say I spent half of it having your husband's penis forced down my throat!!!! An added bonus!! If I allowed him to ejaculate in my mouth, I got 10 pence for sweets. To the mindset of a young child, 10 pence got you a lot of sweets!! Refer back to when Elaine told you how he took every opportunity with Sally. Well, Sally didn't live with him, like I had to. So, just stop and imagine what it was like for me, and you have the audacity to tell me that I should just forget about it and move on because, selfishly, you don't want to keep hearing or thinking about it. All my reactions in life since the abuse have been more than appropriate.

My very first childhood memory was being in the original garage and him bribing me with chocolate to touch his penis. The word willy was used. After all, I was too young to understand the word penis.

My 2nd memory was the one where I tried to tell you what he had done in the garage. You were having none of it and told me never to speak of it again. From then forward, it became the norm in my life to do as he told me. I remember thinking that no one in school spoke of such things happening to them, so therefore, it was like everyone was keeping the same secret, and that is how it was meant to be: a secret. The opportunities for him were endless. Time in the shed alone, time in the garage alone, a wife who had her suspicions but turned a blind eye, car trips alone. Touching me inappropriately whilst I slept.

There was no end to the situation for me, and there was never a place to feel safe. The only times I used to feel safe and know I would be left alone was on those holidays to the Isle of White and Christmases at Bet or June's. Oh, and by the way, I used to wish Bet was my mum; she showed all the characteristics of what I thought a mother should act like. Not you.

You were, and still are, selfish through to the core. As for a father figure, that never ever, ever existed. Just a "monster" that would turn up in the dark and at every corner.

He attempted once to do the full sexual intercourse act, but fortunately, he spared me of that ordeal; otherwise, I would have been damaged for life, given how young I was.

To this day, I remember being pinned to the corner of the bathroom with him contemplating it. A vision, amongst many, that stays etched in my brain.

Coming home with no one else in the house and him making me watch porn on a projector set up in your bedroom. The images were etched on the wardrobes, and they remain etched in my brain to this day.

I remember you saying one of your suspicions was when you caught him in our bedroom for no apparent reason, and he made out he was measuring the window. I remember that incident, and what I see clearly in my mind is the Beano album I was reading, which was dated 1969, which meant I was 7 years old! I would lay in bed, getting as near to the wall as I could to get away from him, and he would say I was making room for him to get into the bed.

The endless promises that he would not do it again to me, only for it to happen over and over again! The mental torture that I had to endure from him and you.

I always remember you saying that there was a fine line between love and hate. I can truly tell you, without a shadow of a doubt, that you have definitely moved into the world of hate for me, and I was a fool not to have gone there many years ago.

The way you have treated me is vile beyond words.

As far as I'm concerned, you are one fucking evil, unbelievable bitch now.

You and Elaine never even flinched at the idea of me being dead.

But dead I'm not, and I intend to fight you all the way now to get justice for myself. Just trying to decide when to

*let Ted, Elaine's place of work, your "fundraising people"
and your neighbours know the truth about you all.*

*Also, seeking a solicitor's advice on suing for historical
child sexual abuse.*

I got no pleasure from finally telling my mother the
unvarnished truth, the graphic details. But she had pushed
me to it, as it was completely obvious that nothing else was
sinking in. And, regardless, I was no longer willing to be
silent.

CHAPTER TWENTY-EIGHT

The Games They Play

My mother never saw it the way I did. To her, every action I took felt like rebellion, a punishment designed to make her suffer. The eleven years I didn't come back? That was my fault in her eyes, my refusal to fall in line. It was easier for her to blame me; after all, I was the one who had stepped away. In these later years, Elaine stayed close and did exactly what she was supposed to. So naturally, I was the problem.

For me, though, it was never about blame. It was about principles, knowing right from wrong and making the difficult choices, even when they hurt. I knew I hadn't done anything wrong. I hadn't abandoned anyone. I hadn't let the past rot away in silence, pretending it hadn't happened. I'd simply done what I had to do, to survive and heal.

Elaine, however, believed money could fix anything. As though all the years of betrayal, silence, and manipulation could be wiped clean with a cheque and a handshake. She even offered me money to stay quiet, convinced that would make everything disappear.

It was almost laughable. I'd always seen right through her, but hadn't realised just how deeply her arrogance ran. The moment I refused to sign that NDA was a turning point, not just for me, but for all of us. It was the moment I saw how she truly operated and the lengths she would go to to protect her carefully built image.

"If there's to be no NDA, then there's no point in me making an offer," Elaine said. Jim and I exchanged glances and replied in unison, "Well, don't make an offer then!" To me, unless you've done something wrong or have things to hide, why would you even want an NDA?

Elaine looked completely deflated, shoulders slumped, head down, unable to believe what had just happened. She wasn't used to being told "no". Then, as if on cue, Mother piped up, "Why don't you want the money?" Elaine exaggerated her response: "Mum, it's not about the money to April. It's about morals and principles."

The tension was palpable, radiating from Elaine. She shifted in her seat, playing the businesswoman she'd always fancied herself to be, calculated, controlled. "Where do we stand?" she asked coldly, as if discussing a business deal rather than family. But that's who she was – someone who believed even loyalty and love could be negotiated.

I could have softened the blow, let her down gently as I had many times before, but something snapped. Years of keeping quiet and walking on eggshells were done.

"We don't stand anywhere," I said. Her face tightened just a little, enough for me to know she realised something had shifted. I wasn't the same person she'd played games with for years. Elaine always believed money was the answer, a tool to control anyone or any situation, but she'd miscalculated. She hadn't expected this new version of me, the one who couldn't be bought.

For Elaine, money was both shield and weapon, how she kept control and stayed on top. If things got messy or emotions complicated matters, she would just sign a cheque and move on. That's what won Sally over. The apple doesn't fall far from the tree. It all clicked, the gut feeling at Christmas that I'd only see Sally once, her expertly deflecting when I mentioned her mother's relationship with money, the emails assuming money was a done deal, calling off the police; it all pointed to a disturbing truth.

But this problem couldn't be solved with money. Just like Father with his pennies, money wasn't going to get them what they wanted this time. What happened in our family couldn't be erased with banknotes and signatures. Some wounds run too deep, and Elaine never understood that. She never would.

I'd spent years watching our family pretend everything was fine, burying secrets and widening cracks. I'd played along, telling myself it was easier to keep the peace, but that time was over. Refusing Elaine's money wasn't just about money; it was about reclaiming my voice, my right to speak up, and my refusal to play their games anymore. That, more than anything, unsettled her.

Out of nowhere, Mother pointed at Elaine, declaring, "And she's the greedy one!" Never had she spoken a truer statement.

Elaine's parting words were, "Do what you like with Mother, as long as you leave Sally and me alone." Hardly the words of someone who cared, despite being Mother's carer.

In 2005, my niece, Elaine's daughter Sally, told her mother that Frank had been abusing her for two years. Elaine didn't tell me until October 2023. As I sat across from Elaine, her hands twisting nervously, her eyes downcast, I could see the truth still shamed her. But it wasn't hers alone; it was shared with Mother, passed down like a cursed heirloom. Neither confronted it properly.

Sally's words to her mother echoed my history, as though I were looking into a mirror and seeing a younger version of myself recounting the same story. I knew the pain, fear, and pressure to stay silent. But the truth always surfaces.

After Sally's drink-driving offence, I'm certain Elaine confronted our parents about nearly losing her daughter's life. The timing aligns too perfectly: by the following year, the Will had changed. What had once been a 50/50 split now left me £100,000, with Elaine receiving the rest, over £1,000,000. A clause stated if I contested the Will, I'd lose even that amount. They saw me as someone to silence and back into a corner.

Elaine had easily convinced our parents, given Mum had washed her hands of me. Another clause stated if anything happened to Elaine before my parents, Sally would inherit everything.

Penny, Elaine's "friend", who lived with her and knew about the abuse, still agreed to be executor of my parents' Will. Interesting choice.

We'd discovered online Sally had been arrested for drink driving, information Elaine hadn't volunteered.

When I asked Mother, "What did our girls do wrong?" Elaine answered for her: "Even though you'd fallen out with Mother, they could've stayed in contact."

"Don't be fucking ridiculous!" My voice cracked, hands trembling. "We protected our girls for years, and that bastard was still around, as if we'd let them near him!" A wave of nausea rose. After all the protection, our girls were being punished for something beyond their control. It was cruel, a deep betrayal.

They justified the unthinkable because they needed Elaine. Our parents were ageing, desperate for someone like her to take charge. Elaine always controlled things, underhanded or not. They kept her happy, gave her what she wanted, and in return, she provided silence and kept Sally quiet. Appearances remained undisturbed.

It wasn't about justice; it was convenience. Easier to give Elaine the bulk and throw me scraps, just enough to keep me quiet. But they underestimated me. I wasn't the same person anymore. Years of silence ended; now it was about fairness.

In the solicitor's office, her words lifted the weight from my chest: "We have a case." It wasn't just about money but finally speaking the truth after years of hiding. The Will tried to control me, but the real victory was reclaiming power taken from me. That was worth far more than £100,000.

Elaine, the counsellor who was supposed to help others find their voice, tried to silence mine. The irony was clear. Her career felt like a reaction, reinventing herself after Sally's abuse. Growing up, Elaine always held the upper hand. She was the golden child, unquestioned.

In the end, it was never about money or inheritance but about morals and principles. Sitting across from the solicitor two days ago, her words resonated deeply: "Morally, you have a case."

The abuse was emotional and psychological, a creeping control stretching decades. What they called loyalty was a chain around my neck that I was finally ready to break.

CHAPTER TWENTY-NINE

Still Trying

When the bungalow was rebuilt, it emerged with a new layout, unfamiliar and unsettling in its own way. The garage door, which Louise and I had once shared the same vivid idea for, was gone. We'd both imagined the same thing, as if we'd plucked the thought straight from each other's minds: the word *PAEDOPHILE* scrawled across it for the world to see. But that vision no longer had a place. The garage had been transformed into an extension of Mother's living room, and where the door had once sat, there was now just another window.

Inside, the original fireplace had somehow survived the fire, standing oddly central to the new living room, as if clinging to its past purpose. It didn't fit, neither in the space nor in the story of this rebuilt home. The area beyond the fireplace felt cold and uninviting, as though it carried the weight of its history into this new chapter.

Maybe it was just me. Maybe it was because I knew it had been his happy place, his sanctuary. And now, it sat there, intruding on the space inside the home, a lingering reminder of what once was.

This is a strange one. After all the harsh words we've exchanged, there's still a quiet little part of me, hidden away but persistent, that likes to believe there's a slim chance for Mum and me to resolve things. To get her to see sense, to somehow move past all the rubble and build something new, something worth remembering. I'm not a religious person, not in the slightest, but I've come to believe in fate. Life has handed me enough twists and turns to make me think it's not all random, and maybe this, this messy, uncomfortable situation, is fate's way of nudging me. Telling me there's still time. Still hope.

Mum can be brutal, that's undeniable. Stubborn too, like trying to reason with a brick wall. But here I am, deciding, choosing, really, to spend time with her. And it's not all for her. No, part of me believes Elaine's pulling her strings, maybe more than ever now that Mum can't really look after herself anymore. And if that's true, if Elaine got her claws in deeper than I thought, then I need to step up.

If I could just have a little more of that mum I glimpsed on my first visit back, the softer version, the one that almost felt like home, it would be something. Something to hold on to. Something to build from. Even if it's just a moment.

"Elaine cooked us all Christmas dinner here when we first returned on the 20th of December. It was lovely," Mum said, her voice warm, almost nostalgic. I could picture it perfectly, Mum glowing with the satisfaction of being back in her bungalow. Sally there too, doting on her first newborn, while I was conveniently out of the picture. The scene practically wrote itself: Mum content, relaxed, free from any complications I might bring. Not just serving up Christmas dinner but likely handing out generous cheques to buy their silence.

I don't comment much, of course. There's no need to start things off on the wrong foot. Instead, I steer the conversation somewhere safer, to Toffee, my little dog. A shared love of animals is one of the few things Mum and I can agree on without tension creeping in.

She chuckles as I recount Toffee's latest antics. It's a laugh that feels familiar, even comforting, like a small window back to the days when we had Cindy. Funny enough, out of all the dogs I've had, Toffee is the closest in character to Cindy – mischievous, cheeky, always up to no good but somehow getting away with it every time. It's the kind of dog that leaves you with endless funny stories, the kind you can't stay mad at for long.

I tell Mum how Toffee is, well… a bit racist. The way she barks at dark-skinned people, whether they're in the street or just on the telly. Mum finds it absolutely hilarious. She laughs in that deep, genuine way I don't hear often enough, and for a moment, it feels good. Good to see her laughing at the right things, to share a little lightness between us for once.

Mum starts talking about her friend Lel, who lives just around the corner. It's one of those stories you couldn't make up, how they grew up around the corner from each other as kids, then reconnected decades later at a jumble sale, only to discover they were neighbours all over again. And now, in their twilight years, here they are, both widows, clinging to life by a thread, keeping each other company one day a week. It's bittersweet, really, like a quiet little circle completing itself.

Then she moves on to the fire, the people who helped, the ones who stepped in when everything was chaos. It's another story that doesn't sit well with me, though I keep my thoughts to myself. I try not to let other people's opinions bother me, but in this case, it's hard. My mind drifts, as it always does when she brings it up. What must those people, those relatives who knew I existed, have thought of me? Did they think I didn't care? That I couldn't be bothered to help? Did they even know I hadn't been told about the fire at all?

I know for sure at least one cousin had the wrong impression. They thought I was in the wrong, that I should have been there to help, like some dutiful daughter swooping in to save the day. It's so easy, isn't it, to jump to conclusions when you don't have the full story? When the truth is locked away in someone else's silence.

Mum speaks with pride about how the villagers raised their hats as his funeral procession passed through the streets. It's a noble image, almost cinematic, but all I can think is, if only they knew. If only they knew the whole truth. If only they knew what I knew.

I mention, briefly, a few people I've been in touch with, but Mum's mind, true to form, immediately goes sniffing for gossip. It's a dangerous path, one I know too well, so I quickly steer the conversation elsewhere. When I deflect, it's to avoid hurting her feelings; when she deflects, it's usually to save her own skin.

To shift the mood, I ask about her baking. "Do you remember when you used to make that apple cake?" Her eyes light up, and without missing a beat, she rattles off the recipe straight from memory, no hesitation, no confusion, just as sharp as ever when it comes to certain things.

I start to tell her about what Emma and Louise have been up to. As it happens, they were both off on some travels when I visited her that day, and I can't help but wonder if it came across like we're always jetting off, living some charmed family life. I try to explain, not that I have to, really, that it's only been like this since Jim retired a couple of years ago. Mum doesn't seem all that interested in the details. To her, it's just another excuse to say, "Oh, well, Emma and Louise seem to be living it up these days," in that casual, barbed way of hers.

We take a little wander to Mum's conservatory, probably the only part of the bungalow untouched by the fire. Now, though, it's become a sort of museum for the things that managed to survive the blaze. On the side, just to the left, on a small ledge sits a small cross-stitch I made for her years ago. I point it out, and she nods vaguely, as though it's just another item among the clutter.

"Did the large picture I sewed for you, of the wildflowers, make it through the fire?" I ask, hesitant but hopeful. She pauses, her face blank, before shaking her head. She doesn't even remember it. The moment stings more than I care to admit.

I always thought her generation, the one that grew up valuing hand-sewn clothes and handwritten notes, would be the type to appreciate the time and care that went into something like that. But no, not in Mum's case. For her, it was just another thing, easily forgotten, another stitch in a tapestry she doesn't even notice anymore.

For years, visiting Mum was like following a script written long before I had a say in the matter. Whether I went to her or brought her to me, it was carved in stone: weekly visits, a whole day set aside, no questions asked. Always letting her choose what we did with the day. It was just what I did, another part of me fulfilling what was expected, what felt obligatory. I didn't think to challenge it.

But with time, and a lot of support, I began to realise it didn't have to be like that anymore. The old rules weren't binding, and I could rewrite them if I wanted. What jolts me awake now, in moments like this, is Jim. Through no fault of his own, he is sitting out in the car waiting for me, a silent reminder that I don't have to stay all day. I've started calling it after a couple of hours, learning to draw the line.

It's liberating, in a way, to see the clock ticking and know I have permission to leave. That I'm not trapped by the old rhythm of expectation.

I tell Mum, as gently as I can, "It's your choice if you want to see me again. Just let Elaine know, and we'll arrange it."

She looks at me, her voice softer than I expected. "I just want it to be like it used to be… but it can't be like that, can it?"

I take a breath, trying to steady myself. "It could be… not quite the same, but maybe a bit like what you remember as the good years. If you could just put your hands up and admit you were in the wrong, things might feel easier. For both of us."

Her face stays impassive, as though the words bounce off some invisible barrier. I wonder if she even hears me, or if she's already replaying some version of the past in her mind, where she's never wrong, and she never has to say sorry.

Somehow, just as I'm getting ready to leave, the subject shifts to the Will. Mum, in her usual offhand way, says, "I don't know why we made that Will."

I pause, keeping my voice even. "Whether you did or didn't, it got made, and you both signed it."

I stay calm and quiet because I'm always determined to leave her on a good note. And today, miraculously, things haven't gone too badly. But something in me won't let the moment pass entirely unchallenged. So I tell her, still measured but firm, "The only way you and him could've been any crueller to me would've been if you'd murdered one of my own. Or murdered me. That's how cruel you've been. Telling me I was to blame for everything; how do you treat someone more vindictively than that?"

Mum doesn't flinch. Instead, her response is as sharp as is probably expected by now: "When you threw me out of the car!"

I want to explode, but I don't. I stay calm, holding on to the composure I've worked so hard to build. I make my way to the door, feeling the weight of everything unsaid pressing down on my shoulders.

And yet, somehow, somehow, we manage to turn it around at the very last moment. By the time I step outside, we've found a sliver of peace to cling to. Her parting words, spoken in a solemn tone that lingers with me long after, are, "See you later, girl."

And just like that, we part ways again.

Weighing up today, it was a strange blend of good and bad, a real patchwork of emotions. For me, there were moments that felt heavy, moments I struggled with, especially towards the end when I laid out my statement. But for Mum? I couldn't help but feel that, apart from hearing those words, she must have enjoyed it. Surely, she had to.

After all, we laughed, we reminisced, we shared something that felt, if not exactly easy, then at least familiar. And yet, even with that thought, there's still this lingering unease, this sense that the scales between us will never quite balance.

CHAPTER THIRTY

Larry Smart's Emails

When I reconnected with Mum after the 11 long years, Christmas was fast approaching. It felt like the perfect time to try and rebuild bridges, not just with her, but with the rest of the family. Why should I stay out in the cold any longer? I'd done nothing wrong. All I had was Larry Smart's address, so I reached out and asked if he could share his siblings' addresses so I could send them Christmas cards.

At that moment, I'd had no intention of sharing my story; it wasn't even on my mind. But as I was gathering those addresses, something shifted. I made the decision to tell my story. I get why it might have seemed calculated, even suspicious, but it really wasn't like that. The timing just made it look that way.

Looking back, perhaps we should have found the other relatives' addresses online, as we did with most of the others, instead of asking Larry. But at the time, it felt natural. Larry was the first relative I opened up to. We had a long phone call, a conversation that was well outside my comfort zone, where I explained everything, including the fact that there was no ulterior motive behind asking for the addresses. He was understanding and compassionate. I even joked with him about how awkward it would be to attend family gatherings with Elaine, and he suggested that we'd probably need to stand at opposite ends of the room.

What I didn't know was that as soon as we got off the phone, Larry called Elaine to confirm if my story was true. I didn't mind; in fact, it seemed reasonable to me.

Not long after, heartfelt messages started arriving from Larry's siblings, full of love, sympathy, and compassion. Ryan even stepped forward, offering to speak on behalf of everyone, including the Thorns, and suggesting we meet up straight away. But I knew better than to rush things. Family dynamics are rarely straightforward, and I suspected not everyone would feel the same. I was right.

I didn't hear anything from the Thorns. Their mother, June, Mum's older sister, was in fragile health, and they didn't want her to know about what I had to say. They didn't want her burdened with the weight of my story, and I understood.

It was after I put my story out there that Sally went to the police, upset that I had included her name. The truth is, it wasn't a choice; it was inevitable. Elaine's failure to act all those years ago left Sally's story entwined with mine. Sally didn't agree with me, but she did understand why things had unfolded the way they had.

Elaine, however, took full advantage of the situation, manipulating and sabotaging my reunion with the family. She probably told the cousins that Sally had gone back to counselling because of me and seemed almost gleeful when she announced that the Smarts had turned against me for bringing Sally's name into it.

To try to repair the damage, we decided to send an email to the Smarts, apologising on Sally's behalf for involving them. Elaine had claimed the police wanted all the addresses of the people I'd shared my story with. I didn't believe her, but just in case, we sent the email.

I received two replies: one from Ryan and one from Larry. Ryan's started with a dismissive, "Oh no, not that subject again." The shift in tone from his earlier messages was staggering. He also mentioned that he knew nothing about the police involvement. Larry, however, began the conversation with more warmth and care than I had expected. His words wrapped around me like a long-lost embrace, and for a fleeting moment, I allowed myself to believe in the comfort of reconnection. But that was my mistake. I had yet to learn that when faced with the full depth of my truth, people often hesitate, retreating, uncertain, unwilling to truly stand in it with me.

From: Larry to April

Subject: Re: Lovely to hear from you!

Hi April,

What a great surprise to hear from you after such a long while. I hope you, Jim, and the girls are all doing well? We've so much to catch up on, we best plan a long chat and a cup of tea…

Please give me a ring whenever you are free, I no longer have a number for you that works. I've tried to call you several times…

Best,
Larry

From: April to Larry

Subject: Re: Lovely to hear from you!

Hi Larry,

Likewise!! I am really excited that you have got in touch and very appreciative of all the addresses that you have passed on to me. Thank you.

I'm pleased to say that Jim, the girls, and I are all well. I hope the same goes for you and yours? We have four adorable grandchildren these days, two grandsons and two granddaughters. How is it possible that we are at the grandparent stage/age now?

Life is hectic this week, but if you could bear with me, I promise next week I will email you to arrange a time to talk on the phone, which I very much look forward to.

Thank you again for getting in touch.

April xx

From: Larry to April

Subject: Re: Lovely to hear from you!

Look forward to catching up next week.

L xx

From: Larry to April

Subject: Contact

Hi April,

I have deliberately started a fresh email. Your last message will be kept confidential/deleted, it is just between you and me.

Of course, I would dearly love to hear from you. You're my cousin, and I've missed you for a long time, even if you get my birthday wrong.

I am so sorry to hear your story. I had no idea of your troubles, and nobody has ever mentioned any detail of your family rift. And nobody has ever spoken badly of you, at least in my earshot, at any family gatherings, where we always ask after you. Your mum and Elaine always tell us how well you are doing.

I am not going to judge anyone or take sides, but I would suggest that you get in touch. Whatever wrongs have happened in the past, it wasn't the wider family's fault, and they don't deserve to be cut off, we all love you too much!

Please call as soon as you're free.

Larry xx

245

From: April to Larry

Subject: Re: Contact

Hi Larry,

I appreciate your confidentiality, but there is no need, unless you want to. I'm quite happy for it to be out in the open now, and if family members want to discuss it, that's fine with me too.

I don't know if you missed the bit where I said I have decided to tell family members? After I sent that email to you today, I posted my story to every family member I could, both sides. I'm hoping this is not a problem for you?

I believe I told you years ago that there was a rift between me and mine. I remember you telling me at the time how your girls didn't want to know you?

I don't believe Elaine or Mum has necessarily spoken badly of me. I have asked them recently what they say to people about my absence, and they just sum it up with "It's a family dispute." Mum tends to add "I don't want to talk about it!" which I imagine is her way of exiting the subject as quickly as possible.

I would like to know though how they know I am doing well these days when they haven't seen or spoken to me for 11 years? This is where it's all so awkward because it's like I'm asking you to either believe them or me while also not wanting to put you in the middle.

You got my birthday right! And I've got to say, it's great to hear the love!

Just want one more confirmation from you, would you like me to phone? If so, I'll do that at 6 pm tonight or tomorrow, whichever suits you best?

Love,
April xx

From: Larry to April

Subject: Contact

YES, please phone!!!

Any time tomorrow is fine. I play in a band and practise each Tuesday evening.

Much love from your favourite cousin,

Larry xx

From: April to Larry

Subject: Re: Contact

Dear Larry,

I hope you and your family are well.

I am writing because, some months back, Sally got in touch and told me that she had reported me to the police for including her name in my letter/story to you. Something I find ironic, Elaine, my mother, and Sally when old enough never reported Frank to the police but saw it fit to report me for telling the truth.

I have since found out that Elaine and Sally had told others about Frank abusing me.

However, the reason for writing is that I have had a conversation with Elaine. She informed me that the police had asked Sally for the names and addresses of the people I had sent letters to and that the police were going to get in touch with them.

Elaine has told me that all the cousins have said to her that "I should never have included Sally in my story/letter." Unfortunately, when Elaine decided to leave Sally with him to be abused, she made Sally a part of my story.

I can only, wholeheartedly, apologise for the police involving you in this matter and for any distress it has caused. I have not heard from the police myself yet, but my understanding is that they still may be in touch.

To continue involving you in this matter was never my intention. I simply wanted to share my truth with you.

Love,
April xx

From: Larry to April
Subject: Re: Contact

Hi April,

I'm on holiday with no internet. I'll get back to you in two weeks.

XX

From: Larry to April
Subject: Re: Contact

Hi April,

I hope all is well with you.

Just before Christmas, I was so excited to be reunited with you, my dear cousin, after so many years. I heard with horror your story and understood your withdrawal from the family. I was looking forward to catching up.

News of your letters was very disappointing and upsetting for me. We had discussed your experiences in confidence, and I assumed that would be reciprocated. You asked me for family contact details to send Christmas cards and greetings to reestablish contact. I did not expect what followed and felt betrayed and misled by your actions. But it is your story, and you are free to tell it as you wish.

I believe your actions did not encourage sympathy for your suffering but rather backfired. It was perceived as "why would you tell tales of your niece?"

Let's start again... Great to have my cousin back. Love and missed you loads. Sorry to learn of your suffering, and I am very keen to help with your healing.

What do we need to do to move forward, unify and unite, forgive, forget, and move on? We can't fix the past and have left it too late to seek justice. So, we either start a new chapter in our lives or let resentment eat us up.

Lots of love,

Larry xx

From: April to Larry

Subject: Re: Matters Passed...

Hi Larry,

I hope you had a nice holiday.

You may wish to re-read the chain of emails, and you will see I never betrayed anyone's confidence. I asked for the addresses to send Christmas cards, which was a genuine intention.

Unfortunately, after visiting my mother and her being particularly nasty to me and failing to show any understanding, I decided to finally tell my story. My aim was never to mislead you, as you put it.

In an email, the night before we spoke on the phone, I explained all this, and I have no recollection of you having a problem with it then, why now?

Whilst on the subject of confidence, why was it that the first thing you chose to do after speaking to me was to phone Elaine and ask her if what I was saying was the truth? When Elaine and I spoke, she told me that she had been in contact with all the cousins to get contact details to give to the police. She also said that all the cousins felt I was wrong to speak out like I had.

Let me be clear: I have no issue with you talking about the subject to whomever you want to, and you have the right to your own opinion. You have the right to speak to Elaine and ask whatever questions you wish, but I find it slightly hypocritical for you to call me out when you have done the same wrong you are accusing me of.

I have only told my mother and Elaine about the love, warmth, and compassion I have received from my cousins and nothing else.

As for "telling tales", as you so cruelly put it, I have only told the truth about what happened to Sally and me. Again, if you re-read your emails, you will see that. However, if you wish to, you can explain to me how it is okay for Elaine to tell Penny about my abuse, it's okay for Sally to tell Paul about my abuse, and I do not know who else they may have told, all without my permission. Yet, when I speak about Sally, I am "telling tales"?

I only emailed to apologise for Sally and Elaine involving others in this exchange, when there clearly was no need. In fact, it should have been them apologising to you and yours, not me.

Like I said, my last email was only to apologise for Sally and Elaine involving you with the police. Whilst I was surprised that she contacted the police, we were and are more than willing to speak to them and give them any copies of correspondence that was sent. I have nothing to hide, and the contents written, again, are only the truth.

There was no need for Elaine to involve the cousins at all, as I would never deny anything I have written or said.

If you knew Elaine how I do, you would see that she didn't like the outpouring of love and understanding I received from all my cousins. Therefore, the only way to stop it was, again, to make me look in a bad light and contact you and yours to gain sympathy for herself. Her manipulation of the whole situation has no bounds.

There was still absolutely no reason for them to have involved you. I am sorry you feel this way.

The manipulation that I have received all my life (from Frank and Elaine) continues. Mum is not so manipulative, she gets slight leeway with me because she is gullible, has always been taken in by them, is easily led, and has little choice these days given her lack of independence. But do not underestimate her capability to tell lies and be nasty, even at 90, to cover herself.

251

Is it any wonder that people like myself, who have to deal with such ordeals in their life choose to keep their mouths shut for so many years and sometimes never speak up at all, for fear of reactions like yours? Down-trodden and afraid to speak out, saying only what people want you to say to protect them or not put them in an awkward position, making everything look "pretty" when it really is not.

I don't expect you to understand, but telling me to "move forward" or "to forgive" are ultimate one-liners straight out of my mother's notebook. "Forget and move on." It is difficult and very upsetting to hear.

I will spare you the details (plus graphic ones), but if you knew exactly what you are asking of me, you wouldn't ask. I said to you on the phone how things would never be right between Elaine and me, and your reply was, "Elaine could stand at one end of the room and I at the other." Where has the "acceptance" within that comment gone?

As for it backfiring on me, as you put it, it was always going to be difficult for you and others, who do not know the full extent of what happened, to understand, as well as what Elaine and Mother still put me through to this day.

Your insinuation is that I was looking for a different result than what was intended. My first email said I didn't want anyone to take sides, and I stand by that. However, your comments clearly show where you stand. That is your prerogative, and I accept that.

I also said I wasn't looking for sympathy and that people should form their own opinion. That was my only intention. There was no ulterior motive, as you allude to.

Another comment out of my mother's notebook: "You can't change the past." No, you cannot, but you can keep on striving to seek understanding and the truth from those involved (Mum and Elaine) and never stop trying to get them to accept their responsibilities and involvement in what happened.

And no, it is not too late to seek justice. There were three people involved in this abuse and the subsequent cover-up of it, as well as the manipulation of me to do as they wished. Until they accept their part in what happened, I will continue to try and make them see the error of their ways.

As for others, I repeat: they can form their own opinions.

I do not and will not experience a built-up "resentment", as you call it. I am aware that my decisions may result in me being seen as the bad guy, but for me, it is more important now, in my healing, that I have self-respect and speak my mind where and when necessary.

This actually leaves me to be a much freer person than I have ever been before in my life. A doormat, I no longer am.

I appreciate your outspoken honesty. I only wish you had spoken sooner about your first issue, as I can't help but feel your built-up resentment contributed to how you felt about my second email.

Lots of love,

April xx

Larry's final email left me fuming, but more than that, deeply saddened. The love I had trusted crumbled under his discomfort. He wanted a tidy resolution, one I was never given. Once again, I was reminded that some wounds are too inconvenient for others to face.

Reconnecting with my mum's side of the family felt like a fragile, precious gift, a glimmer of hope that, maybe, we could mend the broken pieces. For a moment, I allowed myself to believe that honesty might bring us closer. But to have that hope so ruthlessly dashed, not because I lied or hurt anyone, but because I dared to speak my truth, was devastating.

The emotions that followed were overwhelming. At first, there was relief, the kind that comes with finally letting go of a secret held too long. I thought that by opening up, I was giving my family an opportunity to understand me and the pain I had carried for so many years. But that hope quickly gave way to betrayal, the defensiveness, the accusations, and the unwillingness to hear or acknowledge what I was saying. It wasn't just the rejection of my truth; it felt like the rejection of me as a person.

Anger followed, sharp and consuming, as I replayed their responses in my mind. The hypocrisy of those who claimed to value family yet, ultimately, couldn't bear to face the truth about our past. The way they shifted the focus, making it about themselves, protecting their own comfort while leaving me exposed and vulnerable. The refusal to confront the reality of what had happened hurt more than any argument or harsh word.

But underneath the anger, there was something else; for me, there was a quiet resolve. *If their discomfort, their accusations, and their coldness are the price of truth, so be it.* As painful as this experience has been, it reminds me why I must keep speaking out.

This isn't about "he said, she said". It isn't about blame or airing grievances. It's about addressing the truth of what happened to me *as a child* and how it continues to affect my life and relationships.

These exchanges highlight why **so many victims stay silent.** It's not just fear of not being believed; it's the fear of losing everything: love, connection, and the few relationships you hold dear.

The weight of silence is suffocating. For years, I carried that burden, pretending everything was fine, staying quiet to protect others and avoid conflict. Even now, as I try to shed that silence, I see how difficult it is for people to hear. When you speak your truth, you are often met not with understanding but with defensiveness, with people choosing their own comfort over your pain.

But I cannot and will not let that stop me. I will not allow their reactions to dictate my healing. My voice may tremble, and my heart may ache, but I will keep speaking, for myself, for others who are still silenced, and for a future where speaking the truth is no longer met with resistance.

Victim blaming and victim shaming MUST stop!

This issue is about more than my story. It's about how we, as a society, respond to victims. We need to change the way people react when survivors come forward. The discomfort these truths bring cannot outweigh the need for compassion and understanding. We must make space for these stories, even when they are hard to hear. *Especially* when they are hard to hear.

These email exchanges with Larry Smart are a reminder of how much work there is still to do. But they also strengthen my resolve. I will keep speaking, even when it feels like no one is listening. Because this matters. Because victims deserve to be heard. And because change will only come if we continue to tell our stories until silence is no longer the easy option. I have reasons; they only have excuses.

CHAPTER THIRTY-ONE

A Huge Price to Pay

It's July, and I'm headed to a funeral today. The kind that sneaks up on you, not because you didn't know it was coming, but because you never imagined how much it would mean.

It's for Faith, my cousin's wife. We'd only really gotten to know each other in the last couple of months, all through writing. No cups of tea shared, no warm hugs exchanged. Except... there was that one time. Forty-four years ago, at my engagement party. A blur of people in my parents' house, Faith among them. I met her then, fleetingly, but never knew her, not like this.

Faith who, in her darkest moments, shone like a star that refused to be dimmed. Cancer riddled her body, but somehow, when I messaged her, her replies came back like lightning, bright, quick, and full of warmth. She didn't make it about her pain. And I didn't make it about me. Yet there we were, in this peculiar intimacy, two people who'd only just reconnected, with her telling me how much she loved and trusted me. Imagine that. A woman carrying the weight of the world still finding space to carry someone else's heart.

We weren't in the same room, but it felt like we were. The kind of conversations that filled invisible spaces, swelling them with so much love it felt like the walls themselves might burst. Even when she was in the hospital just a couple of weeks ago, she convinced me everything was fine. "Temporary," she'd said, brushing it off like it was just a hiccup. But she never came home.

And now, here I am, stepping into that old cliché: families only come together for weddings and funerals. This one feels different, though. Poignant. Like life itself is tying a knot between joy and pain and asking me to untangle it. I've had moments in my life that blew my mind, times of unbearable joy or searing grief. But this? This feels like both. Like giving birth, in a way. The agony of one life leaving and the joy of another connection born.

At the expense of one remarkable, courageous woman, I feel the rush of family flowing back to me. Forty years of feeling adrift, and now… this tether. How do I even begin to make sense of it? How do you put into words the storm of emotions? The gratitude, the loss, the strange and tender beauty of it all?

Yesterday, just as Jim and I were sitting down to untangle the knot of what we'd do if my mum and Elaine showed up at the funeral, my phone buzzed. A message from my cousin Rachel. No need to feel awkward, it read.

Mum and Elaine hadn't been invited.

I sat there, holding the phone, the weight of those words sinking in. Massive. That's what it was, massive. And then another message followed: they hadn't even told Mum and Elaine about Faith passing and the funeral to prevent any unexpected appearances. For people to believe in me like that, it was big. *Huge.* But I've had to grow into someone strong enough to handle it if they ever change their minds. I've had no choice but to learn to cope with the swings, the reversals.

Still, I couldn't help but feel a flicker of confusion. Why did this side of the family trust my word, my story, when others had questioned and doubted every breath I took? Then again, I know what my sister is capable of. Sabotage comes easy to her.

As we drove, I started calculating how long it had been since I'd seen all these people. Years piled on years until it felt like I was inside one of those *Long Lost Family* episodes I used to watch. Back then, during the 11 years of silence with my mum, I never really felt the pull of those stories. They weren't real to me. Mum wasn't going to come sweeping back into my life, bringing some heart-stopping reunion. But the rest of the family? They hadn't done me any harm. I just... hadn't thought about how I'd feel seeing them again.

We pulled into the cemetery, the car crunching to a stop. I was glad we'd left in plenty of time. This wasn't the kind of thing you arrive late to. Not today.

In the crowd, I spotted a wheelchair and instantly knew it was my uncle Don. Rachel had sent me a photo of him just weeks ago, not that I needed a photo; I would have recognised him a mile off. Jim stopped the car and offered to park while I went ahead. I didn't hesitate. After all these years, there was no time to waste.

As I stood in front of my uncle, my eyes darted to the woman behind his wheelchair. Which one of his daughters was it? There were three. We locked eyes, studying each other, and then it hit us both. The tears came fast and heavy as we fell into each other's arms, holding tight. It was Grace. "Thank you for inviting us today," I said.

"No, no," she said, "you are back, to stay." Her voice was fierce and eager.

Grace turned to her dad and asked him to look at me. At 91, bless him, it took a bit of nudging, but when he realised who I was, his face softened, and warmth radiated out to me like a hug. I moved in and retrieved that warm hug.

I thought about that photo Rachel had sent me. I'd replied with one from our engagement party all those years ago, showing Faith talking to Grace. Rachel had asked, "Who's the girl Faith is with?" and I'd laughed. "It's your sister Grace." Now here we were, laughing about it in person, all those years and connections snapping back into place.

Before Jim even made it back from parking the car, Rachel was in front of me, her face matching the messages we'd exchanged so many times. Then Sarah, the eldest sister. Hugs, embraces, tears, all of it swirled around me like a warm, chaotic storm. Jim's words whispered in my mind: "Let people breathe." But it was overwhelming. Husbands, partners, new generations – they all kept appearing, each introduction a small miracle.

There was so much to take in, so many faces and stories to reconnect with. I wanted to hold on to each moment, to each person, like a lifeline. Honestly, I could have stayed the whole week, soaking in the warmth of family I hadn't felt in decades. And for the first time in so long, I didn't feel like the outsider. I felt like I'd come home.

Just off to the left of the pathway, a familiar face came into view. It was Brenna, my father's youngest sister, the baby of the family. Of the original nine siblings, only she and Rose, who is in a care home, were still alive.

When I was growing up, Mother and Father had little to do with Brenna and her husband, Alex. Out of all the aunts and uncles, Brenna was the one I knew the least. They had two kids, Jules and a son, but I couldn't recall the son's name. They lived fairly close to Aunt Rose and Uncle Don, but we rarely saw them. As I approached, she didn't recognise me right away, but when she clicked, her first words were, "Is your mum here?"

Before I could answer, my cousin cut in abruptly, "No," and walked off. The moment hung awkwardly for a beat. Unlike most of the family, Brenna and Alex hadn't received one of my letters; I hadn't known their address. Quietly, I reassured her that Mum was fine and promised we'd talk later.

When the time came for the family to enter the church first, Brenna's voice rang out with a tone so sharp it cut through the crowd. "Come on, we are family," she ordered, her words brusque but not unkind. It brought a rush of memories, particularly of Aunt Flo, another of Brenna's sisters, who had the same authoritative way about her. I wasn't offended; instead, I felt a quiet warmth in being claimed as part of the fold.

The ceremony itself was deeply moving. It was only during the service that I learned Faith and my cousin Richard had three grown children. How bizarre that I hadn't known! Two beautiful daughters, the spitting image of their mother, and a lovely son who, truth be told, didn't look like either of them. They stood tall and proud, their voices steady as they spoke of Faith, doing her memory justice.

Outside, I embraced Richard, feeling the weight of the years and the grief between us. Amidst the flow of people,

Brenna's son Adam approached. He recognised me instantly. "I saw your mum's face," he said with a wry smile. That face, the one I see staring back at me in the mirror every morning. Unfortunately, it's there.

I struggled to recall his name in the moment. Our childhood connection was faint, but thankfully, Brenna swooped in before I had to admit it, issuing motherly instructions that kept him moving along.

Later, we drove a few miles down the road to the tennis club for the wake. I made a point of finding Brenna again. Her reaction to my news about her brother, my father, was blunt: "It doesn't surprise me."

She never elaborated why.

It was odd; one of the first things she mentioned was something another relative had said recently, on finding out about my story. Both of them remembered my father's flirtation with Ernie's daughter, Lily. Taking into account that Lily was just a teenager at the time. Alex was at the bar while this was being discussed, but when he returned and I shared my story with him, he put his head in his hands, shaking it in despair. And then it came again, the third time I'd heard this little piece of family lore about Father and Lily.

When Alex stepped away, I took the chance to ask Brenna why she and my parents had never gotten along. Her response wasn't an answer, but a wall. The way she held herself and her careful tone screamed that she was keeping something back.

Alex, however, didn't bother with the charade. Without me even asking, he spilt the truth: years ago, their mother had left her inheritance to Brenna, and my parents, along with other family members, had caused a stir about it. The weight of it sat there between us, a piece of ancient family history unearthed at last.

Brenna said nothing, but her silence spoke volumes. Secrets, old wounds, and unspoken resentments had carved their way through the family, leaving gaps I was only now starting to fill.

Quite ironic, really, given how my parents' Will is mapped out. The thought stayed with me as I looked around the room, needing to speak to more people. When the chance came, I walked over to my three girl cousins and found myself slipping into the story I'd been carrying for years. It just came out, naturally, like it had been waiting for this moment.

Grace cut in almost immediately. Without saying much, she grabbed my arm and pulled me off to the side of the room. "Stay put," she told her sisters, her tone firm. I barely had time to process it. What's going on here?

And then she said it: "He done it to me."

I froze. What? I couldn't even form a proper response, just a jumble of thoughts and disbelief. The way she said it knocked me off balance.

Grace carried on, her voice calm but deliberate. "Your mum and dad loved to throw a party. They were always good parties. As young children, we were allowed our first little tipples of alcohol."

Her words were like a stone dropping into the middle of my chest, sending ripples through everything I thought I knew. I felt myself standing there, rooted in place, yet somehow detached from the moment. A brief, unwelcome vision, painted by her words, pulsed behind my eyes.

The room felt smaller, quieter, like the air had shifted. I watched her face, trying to process what she'd just shared, what it meant, not just for her, but for me, for everything. And as she spoke, I knew this wasn't just a conversation. It was a moment, the kind that changes *everything.*

"I was only eight years old, and I was tired, so I took myself up to one of the bedrooms to have a little nap. All of a sudden, I am woken by your dad trying to put his hand in my knickers. I told him to get off and pushed him away. I was straight off downstairs to tell my mum and dad what he had done, in front of everyone. Their reaction was to say, 'no, darling, you are imagining it.'"

Worse than Grace's revelation was the fact that my mother, witnessing the commotion of Grace telling her parents what he had done, responded with a dismissive coldness: *"He wouldn't do anything like that!"*

The sting of my mother's words, as Grace reported them, was sharper than I'd expected. This was the same woman I had once confided in about what my father had done to me, the same woman who had admitted her own suspicions years ago. And yet, as Grace recounted, she had once again chosen denial, preferring the comfort of disbelief over the weight of the truth.

Strangely, as Grace told me this, a memory surfaced. I recalled walking into the room just as my mother was speaking, catching only the tail end of her words. At the time, I hadn't realised what had just unfolded – that Grace had been telling her parents everything. I hadn't made the connection. But now, with the full story in front of me, it hit me harder than I could have imagined.

I stood there, absorbing what I'd just heard. Grace is four years younger than me, which meant I'd have been only twelve when it happened to her. I'd spent a lifetime believing I was alone in this nightmare, that I was his sole target. But recently learning about Sally's abuse, and now, standing face to face with this harsh reality, I saw it clearly; there was now yet *another* victim. My own cousin. Yet another innocent life scarred by my father, the bastard. Now there are three children that we know of who had been sexually molested by that monster. All members of his own family! Who else had suffered at the hands of this sick excuse for a human?

Grace, meanwhile, kept apologising to me, again and again, as though she'd somehow wronged me. But there was nothing to forgive; she hadn't done anything wrong. She told me her father, Don, had spent 11 years wondering aloud, "I don't understand why they don't have anything to do with April."

Grace had known the reason all along but had never said a word.

I couldn't blame her for it. How could I? She had her own demons to wrestle, and her own battles to fight. At the time, I appreciated Grace's honesty, but it wasn't until a few days later, when I'd had time to process everything, that I realised she was right. If she had spoken up during those eleven years, it might have caused her mum some upset, but with me behind her, we could have brought him to justice. Like Mother, Elaine and Sally, Grace had denied me that opportunity.

Grace said it was okay for me to share her story, that my father had sexually abused her, just as Richard had done, allowing me to tell Mum about Faith's passing.

A funeral seemed the strangest setting for this kind of heartfelt connection, but it felt right nonetheless, like being drawn gently into the movements of a dance I was just beginning to accept.

The music started, so we took ourselves outside. I found a spot on the step and sat between my two cousins, Sarah and Grace. Even amid the seriousness of our conversation, somehow, we managed to laugh. Their sibling banter was electric, bouncing effortlessly back and forth, a rhythm they'd perfected over years of closeness. Watching them, I felt a sharp, familiar sting, a longing for the kind of connection I'd never known with my own sister. How wonderful it must be, I thought, to have someone who truly understood you, who shared your history without judgement or rivalry. It was a closeness I'd often dreamed about but had always remained painfully out of reach.

Then came Adam. I'd forgotten his name, but his face was very familiar, just as mine was to him. After saying hello and hearing of his curiosity, I shared a brief version of my story with him. Like everyone else, he was kind, sympathetic, and full of apologies for what I had been through. It had been so interesting listening to everyone's life stories. Numbers were exchanged – lots of them. I hoped, truly, that I could find a way to balance all these reconnections going forward.

Next was Uncle Don. At ninety-one, firmly parked in his wheelchair like a king holding court, he was the last person I approached that day. Before I could even say hello, he cut straight to the chase, eyes sharp and voice unwavering. "I never want to set eyes on your mother again," he declared bluntly, with no room for argument.

He wasn't finished. Leaning in closer, as if sharing a secret he'd waited far too long to reveal, he continued, "Every time the family asked after you, she'd snap, 'Don't talk to me about that girl; I've done nothing wrong to her, but she wants nothing to do with me!'"

His words struck hard, nothing like the carefully sanitised version Mum had fed me. Uncle Don shook his head, disgust etched clearly across his weathered face. "Conveniently left out what your dad did, didn't she? And let me tell you, he did it to my Grace, too!"

The weight of his words left me slightly stunned. If Grace hadn't chosen to tell me earlier, I would have had no choice but to find her and demand the truth myself. Luckily, we had been spared that situation. We said our goodbyes, and Grace, especially, was most insistent that we meet up again.

The day felt impossibly short. There weren't enough hours to soak it all in. I didn't want it to end, but Toffee, my little dog, was waiting at home, and we had to think of her. Regardless, the warmth of the day lingered. Everyone had been so kind, so loving.

As we left the venue, I unexpectedly ran into a distant relative I hadn't seen in years. In a quiet moment, they confided in me that Don had doubted my story at first. It wasn't until someone reminded him of his own daughter Grace's abuse by Frank that he finally believed me. I believe it's unlikely he had forgotten; he just hadn't believed Grace until now.

That was interesting, I thought. I then told my relative that Don himself had shared Grace's story with me earlier that same day.

As we crossed the car park, reality caught up with me in the form of sore feet. The new shoes I'd been wearing had been rubbing all day, but I'd been so absorbed in everything else, I hadn't noticed until now. It hit me then, how wise it had been to let Jim do the driving. My body and mind were beyond exhausted.

When we finally got home, I was overwhelmed by the simplest decisions. Do I go to the toilet first? Change into my nightwear? Get a drink? Eat something? None of it mattered. All I wanted was to let my head hit the pillow and let sleep take over. The day had been long, emotional, and utterly draining. Yet, as I lay in bed, one thought brought a gentle flicker of hope: Grace and I had talked about staying in touch. It felt like the beginning of something positive, a fresh chapter, maybe even the sisterly connection I'd always yearned for.

But as days passed, it became abundantly clear that Grace had a change of heart about staying in contact. She only replied to one of my messages and then went silent on me. Whatever her reasons, her silence hurt, leaving me with that familiar ache of loss once again.

A few days later, I was texting my cousin Rachel. Midway through our conversation, she casually asked if Grace had mentioned that she (Rachel) had witnessed what my father had done to her in the bedroom that night. I stared at my phone, stunned.

"No," I replied, my fingers frozen over the screen, unsure how to respond. I could hardly believe yet another piece of family history was surfacing like this. Rachel explained that she was only four years old when it happened. She and some other children had been playing hide-and-seek upstairs and were hiding under a bed when my father came into the room and sexually abused Grace. Unlike my sister, who had been fifteen at the time, Rachel had been far too young to understand it, yet the memory had haunted her ever since.

As an adult, Rachel became a single mother herself and was fiercely protective of her daughter. She refused to let her parents babysit if my parents were visiting. Eventually, when Rachel was around twenty, she confronted Grace about what she'd witnessed. I suspect it's remained their secret ever since.

Rachel didn't stop there. She went on to tell me something else; that their other sister, Sarah, had no idea about Grace's story. I'd assumed, wrongly, that their closeness in church, the way they clung to each other, meant they were a tightly knit family. But now I realised how much I didn't know. How fragile these connections might be. How carefully I'd have to tread if I wanted to truly be accepted into this fold.

That's the thing about being out of the loop for so long. You think you're stepping back into something familiar, but really, you're walking into a maze of lives you haven't been part of, stories you don't know and relationships you can't yet read.

The truth is, I won't be able to keep up with the complexities of all this forever. It's too tangled, too messy, too layered. But one thing is clear: if it hadn't happened to that family, if it hadn't been part of *their* story, they might well have doubted me, just like Mother's family has. Left to my uncle alone, I would have been dismissed completely. And yes, Grace's parents should have listened to her when she was eight . The era shouldn't matter; parents have a responsibility to listen to their children.

I decided to withdraw from all the family I met back up with at the funeral. Not because I do not want to be part of the family, but because I do not want to be the cause of a family rift within their family. I feel they are keeping me at arm's length, maybe for the same reason.

Not only was my so-called father extremely sick and evil, he also left one huge trail of destruction behind him. A legacy of sheer carnage that continues to leave me ostracised by the vast majority of my family.

Over the years, I've read countless stories about sexual abuse, each one illuminating the same painful truth: victims are rarely believed and often ostracised. I thought I'd prepared myself for this inevitability. But nothing could have braced me for the cruelty of it.

At first, people seem to get it. Their compassion feels genuine, their understanding palpable. And then, just as you begin to believe you're being seen and heard, they snatch it all away. It's a kind of rejection that cuts deeper than the initial disbelief.

But I'm not who I used to be. I've grown strong enough to weather this. To rise above the wrongs done to me. To hold my truth, even when others can't.

CHAPTER THIRTY-TWO

More Secrets

Years ago, when I used to visit my mum, she would often tell me how Elaine was taking advantage of her and Father. She shared stories about Elaine bringing her dogs to them when they were practically at death's door, leaving them to cope, whilst Elaine went on holiday or even dropping her shoes off for Mum to shine. At the time, I would listen and sympathise, but when I remind her of these occasions now, she acts as though I've made it all up.

However, as I sit in her living room, after the funeral, a dog crate in the centre of the room provides undeniable proof. Apparently, at 91, Mum has been puppy-sitting for Sally while she went on holiday. She brushes it off, as though it's perfectly normal, but I can't help thinking it's just another example of her refusing to acknowledge how much Elaine has taken advantage of her over the years.

I take a deep breath and ask, "What happened to Grace, Mum?"

The moment I mention Grace's name, Mother flies into attack mode. "You've obviously been round raking up dirt," she accuses.

I can't help but think it's a bit strange. If she has no idea what I'm talking about, why react like that?

I tell Mother about Grace, and she immediately sounds cagey. It rolls off her tongue too easily. "Did she not tell her mum and dad?" she asks, shunning any responsibility.

She goes on to say, "I went to stay with Rose for a few days once, when your dad and I fell out, over him having an affair, you know? I went to tell Rose something."

I know instinctively what she's referring to; she doesn't need to spell it out.

"But Rose cut me short." Like some unwritten law within their friendship. "Some things are best left unsaid," she reminded Mother. "Like secrets that only best friends keep."

In one foul swoop, Mother reneges on her promise to Rose and throws her under the bus, making it sound like it's all Rose's fault. She knows full well that Rose has no voice these days and can't defend herself, trapped in the advanced stages of dementia.

I tell her what I've been holding in for years: that she needs to take responsibility for silencing me all this time. Instead of feeling punished because I recently shared my story with relatives, she should be thankful I couldn't have told them 30 years ago. Back then, I had no voice because she made sure of it. But Mum refuses to see it this way.

"You should've said something when your father was alive," she says flatly, "so he could have taken the brunt of it, instead of me."

"Easy to say now," I reply, frustration tightening in my chest. "You wouldn't have said that then, and you know it."

I go on to tell Mother about Faith's funeral, which we attended this week. She's taken aback; it's the first she's heard.

When I mention that I haven't seen these relatives for forty years, she tells me that's my fault. As far as she's concerned, all I had to do was lie about what happened.

"You know what, April – you're ill!" Mother says.

"No, I'm not ill. You just can't stand it that I've found my voice."

Suddenly, she pipes up, in a fit of anger, "I wanted to cut you completely out of the Will, ya know? But I was talked out of it by Elaine."

And there it was, Mother admitting Elaine's influence over changing the Will(s). This clearly shows Elaine's control over both Mother and Father. As far as Mother was concerned, I was to end up with whatever Elaine dictated.

Referring to Father, my mother goes on to say that "she believes everyone should be given three chances".

Very convenient, given he had *three* victims, that we know of.

For a moment, she sits quietly. Then, in one of her rare moments of admission, she says, "He was going to do what he wanted to do." She isn't talking about any specific moment, but I know exactly what she means. She's talking about the abuse, that she couldn't stop him, that she loved him and wasn't willing to leave him.

It blows my mind. What planet is she on? Mum genuinely believes that most people would have made the same choice if they were in her position. I can't fathom it, and I can't accept it, but there she is, sitting across from me, unwavering in her belief.

CHAPTER THIRTY-THREE

Survival

Just this morning, I shared the chapter I'd written about "home discomforts" with one of my daughters. We were sitting in Costa, sipping our coffees, the usual buzz of the café surrounding us. I never expected her reaction. Before she even finished reading, tears welled up in her eyes, and she broke down, right there in front of me. I hadn't meant to upset her; I hadn't meant to drag her into my past, but as she cried, she looked at me and said something that will stay with me forever: *"They did that to you, Mum."*

Her words hit me like a wave, but not in the way you might think. I saw the anger in her eyes, fury, not just for what I went through, but for all the ways it had been ignored, covered up, brushed aside. She was furious, about everything I had carried alone, as a child. As a mother herself of two young daughters, someone who tries to see the good in everyone, she couldn't hold back her rage. She shouted, right there in the middle of the café, about how much she hated them, my parents, for all of it. And she didn't care who was watching or listening. In that moment, I felt something stir in me.

Her anger, her fire, suddenly gave me a strength I didn't know I had. I could not handle seeing my daughter so enraged and upset. It was one thing them trying to destroy me, but I would not allow that same pain to be bestowed on my children. These feelings alone left me wondering, how on earth did Elaine not want Father convicted after finding out what he did to her own daughter? Somehow, I needed to turn this into a positive. It became second nature from any early age to be resourceful. Then it came to me; her actions suddenly gave me the courage to face the hardest part of my past, to confront the way I had survived as a child. A resourcefulness I used back then. It's a truth I've kept buried for so long, but not anymore. It's part of my story, but it no longer defines who I am.

Who teaches a child the meaning of words like *abuse* or *molestation*? No one ever did. It was the same when I started my period. My mum barely explained what was happening; she just spat out the words "You are like that" in such a disgusted tone, as if I were something degrading and dirty. I can still hear her voice now, the way it carried that low, almost growling edge of shame. It made me feel as though I'd done something wrong simply by growing up.

If it hadn't been for having an older sister and sharing a bedroom, I'd have believed I was dying, or that somehow, everything that had happened to me had damaged me beyond repair. Mother used that terminology, "Oh, you are like that", forever after.

But there was something I learnt on my own, even though no one ever spoke of it. A child, no matter how young, can experience physical sensations. I suppose most people believe that sort of thing only happens after puberty. I wish I could have been one of those people. But for me, it became a part of my *survival;* I didn't know it as shameful or embarrassing, until I learnt what sexual abuse was and then it's been my "shame" and "embarrassment" to carry ever since. And admitting this, here and now, feels like finally laying down a burden I've carried for too long. I can't bear the weight of it anymore. It *wasn't* my fault; it never was. This was just the way I coped with the situation I was trapped in. When you're a child, caught up in things you shouldn't have to endure, you have no choice but to grow up quickly, too quickly. And I guess this was about my way of doing that.

Father gave me a book with some explicit details in. He told me to "hide it" because it was "our secret". He said it was "a magic book".

Every time my mum told me she was working that evening, a knot of dread would tighten in my stomach. The air around me would grow heavier, as though it, too, understood what was coming. I'd scurry to grab the book I kept hidden beneath my dolly's mattress in the carrycot, my little secret sanctuary. That book was my refuge, my way of escaping for a few stolen moments. I'd hide the book under my clothing and retreat to the bathroom, the only room in the house with a lock on the door. I sat behind that door and read for a while. It was the one place where I could pretend to feel safe. I didn't entirely understand why I needed those moments, but I only knew that, somehow, they made everything he was going to make me endure a little easier to bear.

But there were times when I wasn't quick enough, when I didn't have the chance to retreat to my safe space. On those days, it felt like the walls were closing in. I can't describe it any other way; those moments felt like I was drowning, as if the world had abandoned me to fend for myself. Powerless. That's the only word for it: completely and utterly powerless, like living in a total nightmare you cannot wake up from.

CHAPTER THIRTY-FOUR

How Could a 'Mother 'Be So Cruel?

I tell Mum that I've been to the police, as advised by my solicitor and suggested by my cousin Sarah, though I didn't tell her the last bit. Mother's reaction is immediate and furious. She accuses me of playing a dirty trick on her, her voice sharp and unforgiving. "You're sick, girl, you are. I think you're very sick," she says, her words like daggers. Then, as if to twist the knife further, she adds, "I only have one daughter I care about, and I don't want to see you anymore."

I try to stay composed. "You should be pleased for me," I tell her, my voice steady but my heart pounding. "I've finally found my voice."

My heart tightens with tentative hope as I open my book to the same passage Emma read in Costa. I secretly long for her approval, foolishly hoping she might finally see my truth, perhaps even acknowledge my courage. But Mum's reaction is not one of pride or encouragement. Instead, she looks at me with cold disdain and declares, "You're a spiteful bitch now."

Most mothers would feel proud if their child wrote a memoir, proud of the courage it took to tell their story. A mother with nothing to hide would encourage it and even celebrate it. But not my mother. She knows what my book will expose – the decades of cruelty, the neglect, the silence she enforced. And that terrifies her. This book won't just be my story; it will lay bare the truth about her and the things she's spent years hiding from the world.

She looks at me, her face twisted in anger, and asks, "Why did you come back?"

"Because I hoped you'd see the light by now," I reply honestly.

But there's no light to see. She begins ranting, her voice rising as she spirals into delusion. Then, suddenly, the words that leave her mouth knock the air from my lungs: "You probably enjoyed it!" she says.

I stare at her, disbelief and rage bubbling under my skin. Her words hang between us, ugly and twisted, and it made me feel physically sick. For a moment, I'm frozen, my breath shallow, my heart hammering with the sheer brutality of her accusation. It's one of those moments that fractures something deep inside, a boundary crossed, never to be mended.

"I beg your pardon?" I ask.

And then, as if to add insult to injury, she continues, her voice dripping with venom: "Thank you, April. How nice of you to rape my husband. I don't want you here. Just stay away. I'm sick and tired of the subject, and you're just not letting it go."

I feel my will to endure any more crumble. How could she say something so unbelievably monstrous? But despite the exhaustion and despair clawing at me, I make a decision. I will leave, but not on her terms. I need her to see that the old April, the one who let them bully, coerce, and manipulate her, no longer exists.

So I stay calm and deliberate, feeling strength rising with every passing second. Yes, it's her house, but my dignity no longer belongs to her. I've reclaimed it piece by piece. And when I walk out that door, I leave as the person I've fought so hard to become: a woman who refuses to ever be silenced again.

CHAPTER THIRTY-FIVE

Full Circle

Within a week of my last visit to my mother, I felt it happen. I was back in that deep, dark hole again.

Like a ball of wool being rolled across the floor at full speed, I began to unravel. It was all happening so quickly, and there wasn't a pause button in sight. No way to take stock, no chance to pull myself back together. That's the thing with the deep, dark hole; it doesn't wait for you. It sucks you in faster than you can blink.

I never imagined I'd end up here again. But here I was, and it wasn't just the feeling. No, this time, it was like I'd been handed a front-row seat to relive how I felt during the first 20 years of my life. There was no searching my mind for it; the memories were all too clear.

Mother had done it again. *Bravo, Mother!* Just when I thought I'd grown strong enough to handle whatever she threw at me, she found a way to catch me off guard, even at 61 years old. She always does. After all the cruelty she's dished out, I thought by now it would just bounce off me. But somehow, with one fleeting moment, she managed to get in under my skin.

I'm out of words to describe her. She is the complete and utter pits. I suppose, without even realising it, I'd been waiting for a sign that it was time to walk away. And now, here it was. Not a whisper, but a punch.

There was no more "us". The truth is, there had never been an "us" to begin with. This was my moment to finally accept it and move on.

It's hard to put into words how she made me feel with those parting words. The bleakness of it. The way it left my head heavy and tangled, unable to string two coherent thoughts together. Simple tasks became impossible. I couldn't even drag myself away from the mirror, feeling a compulsive need to pick myself apart.

It's the coldest, darkest, loneliest place to be. And when you're there, all you can do is use one word, if you can manage it. That word is "help".

Yet, in that bleak moment, I didn't immediately realise help was already within my reach. Initially, the darkness felt overwhelming, too vast, too heavy. How could I possibly offer encouragement to others when I was barely afloat myself? That shift didn't happen overnight. First, I had to allow myself the grace of acknowledging my own pain, to sit with it, understand it, and gently ease myself towards healing. It was only through that slow, cautious process, one small step after another, that I found myself rediscovering the strength I'd forgotten was always there.

Gradually, I remembered that I'd been here before, and each time I'd found a way back. Each time, I'd come out a little wiser, a little more resilient. The supportive voices of my nuclear family echoed louder, reminding me I wasn't as alone as I'd believed in those dark moments. They became my mirrors, reflecting strength back at me until I could see it for myself.

Only then did I begin to understand the power of connection, the necessity of support, and the courage it takes to ask for help. Slowly, gently, I started feeling the urge to pass that strength forward, to speak up, even if my voice trembled, knowing that someone out there might need these words just as much as I once did.

Writing this book has given me my voice back. It has allowed me to reclaim my story, my truth, and to finally step out from beneath the shadows of the past. I am no longer silenced or held captive by experiences I didn't choose. Through sharing my journey, I've rediscovered a sense of purpose, and most importantly, a renewed belief in myself.

Thankfully, my family, my small, wonderful family, has always been there for me. My two sons-in-law included, they've always rallied around me and kept me out of harm's way. But this time, I had something extra: the advice I'd received from the police, of whom I must say were amazing. Two women police officers, one a detective sergeant, came to my home within a day of reporting the crime. They showed great sensitivity, believed me, and treated the case as though it happened just yesterday.

They had linked me to a helpline, and at first, part of me thought I was too old for this, too far gone. But then I thought, What have I got to lose? And I was so glad I gave it a chance.

The helpline turned out to be a lifeline. One of the first things they taught me was about hindsight and how it can be a trap. That lovely woman on the other end of the line told me to leave hindsight at the door. I'd carried so much regret over the years, so much self-blame for speaking up too late. Her words stayed with me, and slowly, I began to let go.

I learnt about boundaries. Real boundaries. And, especially, how not to let evil people like them manipulate me anymore. It was like being handed a new set of tools to navigate life. And this time, with their help, I climbed out of that dark hole quicker than I ever had before.

Looking back, if the family had agreed to counselling with me all those years ago, I might not have struggled so much along the way.

We all have to find our own way of dealing with things; there's no single path to healing, no perfect roadmap to follow. But if you're out there, carrying the weight of it all, feeling exhausted by the mental and emotional load, I want you to hear this: you are not alone. You are not broken. And you do not have to figure this out on your own.

Even if you're not ready to share your story, even if speaking about it feels impossible right now, please, don't stay trapped in silence. At the very least, reach out for help in a way that feels manageable to you. Find a therapist, join a support group, and read books by those who have walked this road before you. If professional counselling feels out of reach, look into charities and online resources; there are free and low-cost options out there. Many crisis lines and mental health organisations offer support via text or chat if speaking feels too overwhelming.

Healing isn't just about talking; it's about gaining the tools to process what you've been through, to reframe your thoughts, and to slowly release what has felt impossible to carry alone. It can take time, but the right support can change everything. A good therapist or mentor can help you navigate the past, understand your triggers, rebuild your confidence, and set boundaries so you can reclaim your life.

And through it all, please recognise your own resilience. You have survived things that no one should have to endure. *Yet, you are still here.* That in itself is extraordinary! You are already stronger than you know, not because of what happened to you, but because of how you have kept going. Honour that strength. Honour the part of you that refused to give up, even in the hardest and darkest moments.

Most importantly, know this: *you are not what was done to you.* You are not the version of yourself that your abusers tried to shape. They do not get to define you. You get to decide who you become. And I promise you, there is hope. There is healing. When all feels lost, there are people who will stand beside you, listen to you, and believe you.

Please, reach out. Take up space. Use your voice in whatever way feels right for you. You are worthy of help, of support, and of peace. You are worthy of a future that is no longer shaped by your past. Be open-minded and learn from other people's mistakes and therefore try and find the strength to come forward sooner so that something can be done about it.

And now, as I finish this book, I feel like I've found some closure. This process has enabled me to untangle what the vast majority of my life has been about, and now I'm ready to *let it go* and carry on with life with the same outlook as I had in the golden years; free and eager to enjoy life to its fullest again.

Mother, you said that I wasn't *ambitious*.

Well, I think this book proves otherwise.

www.ingramcontent.com/pod-product-compliance
Ingram Content Group UK Ltd.
Pitfield, Milton Keynes, MK11 3LW, UK
UKHW041825210925
463146UK00004B/9

9 781918 038682